SpringerBriefs in Criminology

For further volumes:
http://www.springer.com/series/10159

Lorraine Mazerolle • Elise Sargeant
Adrian Cherney • Sarah Bennett
Kristina Murphy • Emma Antrobus • Peter Martin

Procedural Justice and Legitimacy in Policing

Springer

Lorraine Mazerolle
Institute for Social Science Research
University of Queensland
St Lucia
Queensland
Australia

Kristina Murphy
School of Criminology and Criminal Justice
Griffith University
Mt Gravatt
Queensland
Australia

Elise Sargeant
Institute for Social Science Research
University of Queensland
St Lucia
Queensland
Australia

Emma Antrobus
Institute for Social Science Research
University of Queensland
St Lucia
Queensland
Australia

Adrian Cherney
School of Social Science
University of Queensland
St Lucia
Queensland
Australia

Peter Martin
Operations Support Command
Queensland Police Service
Brisbane
Queensland
Australia

Sarah Bennett
Institute for Social Science Research
University of Queensland
St Lucia
Queensland
Australia

ISSN 2192-8533 ISSN 2192-8541 (electronic)
ISBN 978-3-319-04542-9 ISBN 978-3-319-04543-6 (eBook)
DOI 10.1007/978-3-319-04543-6
Springer Cham Heidelberg New York Dordrecht London

Library of Congress Control Number: 2014931689

Printed on acid-free paper

Springer is part of Springer Science+Business Media (www.springer.com)

Acknowledgements

The authors would like to acknowledge the funding and in-kind support from the Australian Research Council (ARC) Centre of Excellence in Policing and Security (CEPS), the Institute for Social Science Research (ISSR) at the University of Queensland, the Queensland Police Service (QPS), the UK National Policing Improvement Agency (NPIA), George Mason University (USA) and the Campbell Collaboration. We note that the NPIA and George Mason University provided funding, respectively, for the systematic search and systematic review on legitimacy in policing. CEPS provided funding for the Queensland Community Engagement Trial (QCET), with Queensland Police providing enormous in-kind support and goodwill to implement the trial. Support and review guidance from the Campbell Collaboration (especially Professor David Wilson, Professor David Weisburd and Dr Charlotte Gill) is acknowledged, along with the extensive comments provided by the Campbell Collaboration reviewers for the title, protocol and final report. This monograph draws heavily from the authors' collective experiences of both the research processes and findings of the systematic search, the systematic review and QCET.

In addition to the in-kind support provided by the QPS, we acknowledge and thank specific members of the QPS for their leadership throughout QCET, in particular Assistant Commissioners Peter Martin and Ann Lewis, Kim Adams, Deputy Commissioner Brett Pointing, Commissioner Ian Stewart, Superintendents Tonya Carew, Ron Cooper and Tony Rand, Inspectors Pete Hosking and Shaun Dinon, and Senior Sergeants Stephen Peck and Neale Stonely. We thank these members for all of their support for QCET above and beyond the call-of-duty both during the development and then implementation of QCET. We also appreciate the efforts of the Metropolitan South Region traffic officers who took part in the trial. We note that the views expressed in this material are those of the authors and are not those of the Queensland Police Service. Responsibility for any errors of omission or commission remains with the authors. The Queensland Police Service expressly disclaims any liability for any damage resulting from the use of the material contained in this publication and will not be responsible for any loss, howsoever arising, from use or reliance on this material.

The production of this monograph as well as the work that went into QCET, the systematic search and the systematic review would not have been possible without a small army of dedicated research staff. The authors thank (in alphabetical order) Sarah-Ann Burger, Jacqueline Davis, Elizabeth Eggins, Patricia Ferguson, Dr Angela Higginson, Linzie Jones, Dr Matthew Manning, Professor Kerrie Mengersen, Dr Silke Meyer, Jen Owens, Jegar Pitchforth, Phyllis Schultze, Adele Somerville, Dr Gentry White, Harley Williamson and Renee Zahnow. Finally, we thank Professor Cynthia Lum for providing the opportunity for us to put together this monograph.

Contents

List of Figures

List of Tables

Chapter 1
Why Police Should Care About Procedural Justice and Legitimacy

Introduction

Police across the world are generally familiar with the concepts of procedural justice (PJ) and police legitimacy. Academy training, promotion courses, in-service training, and university or college education of police contain modules and classes that explicate the principles of PJ and describe the importance of legitimate authority. The terminology might be different in different arenas and the learning might be explicit or implicit, but the basic ideas and concepts are, for the most part, universally taught across the range of training and education opportunities offered to police. Indeed, when the Queensland Community Engagement Trial (QCET) team at the University of Queensland (see Mazerolle et al. 2011a) began talking to traffic police about PJ (see Chap. 4), it was not uncommon for the police to remind the research team that the basic principles of PJ are sprinkled all over recruit and in-service training. However, we suggest more can be done to incorporate the principles of PJ into all types of police–citizen interactions.

Our book explores how police can systematically put PJ into practice and subsequently improve legitimacy. Easy? It could be. But our systematic review of the extant literature on PJ and police legitimacy, coupled with our experience with QCET, seems to suggest that it is easier said than done. So, the goals of our book are to make the case for why PJ and legitimacy matter to police (Chap. 1), identify the different ways that police tactics can be adapted to do more PJ (Chap. 2), highlight the outcomes of different PJ police interventions (Chap. 3), introduce and discuss QCET, particularly focusing on the actual dialog content of PJ (Chap. 4), identify the things police liked (and disliked) about doing PJ within the context of QCET (Chap. 5), describe the barriers that work against implementing PJ in policing (Chap. 6), and then draw to conclusion with a discussion as to how PJ might be rolled out more broadly within policing across the world (Chap. 7).

In the remainder of this chapter, we define PJ and police legitimacy and then provide ten basic reasons why PJ and police legitimacy matter to police. We created these top ten reasons from the academic literature and packaged it in a way, we hope, that makes the case as to why police should be convinced that doing PJ will, ultimately, improve the practice of policing. We readily acknowledge that it is

L. Mazerolle et al., *Procedural Justice and Legitimacy in Policing*,
SpringerBriefs in Criminology, DOI 10.1007/978-3-319-04543-6_1,

not always easy to do PJ—if it was easy, then police would universally do PJ and not struggle with applying its principles to everyday policing. We also recognize that a lot of what the police do already is like "old wine in new bottles": The key principles of PJ have been part of frontline policing for years. Hopefully, then, our top ten reasons for why PJ and police legitimacy matter to police will strike the right balance between (1) increasing awareness by communicating what we know (and police might already know) from the academic literature on PJ and police legitimacy, (2) generating acceptance by making the case to practitioners that the findings might actually be good to implement, and (3) facilitating adoption by stimulating a desire among police to put the theory into practice. D.A. Davis and Taylor-Vaisey (1997) describe this process as the three As: awareness, acceptance, and adoption. We hope that this book in its entirety—and this chapter in particular—can make some headway toward making police more aware about the "doing of PJ," more willing to accept PJ as the best way to engage with people, and more likely to adopt the principles of PJ in all aspects of police practice.

Defining PJ and Police Legitimacy

Police already explicitly or implicitly incorporate the principles of PJ into police practice and we imagine all policing organizations consider they are legitimate. But what do academics mean by PJ and police legitimacy? What is the link between these concepts? And what does academic research say about how police can utilize PJ to improve legitimacy? In a recent academic paper, Jackson et al. (2012, p. 1) define legitimacy as "the right to rule and the recognition by the ruled of that right." In this way, even though policing organizations are given the right to rule by the state, legitimacy only exists when it is perceived by the public. When measured in research, legitimacy traditionally captures the degree to which ordinary citizens have trust and confidence in authorities and are willing to obey the directives of these authorities (Tyler 2005). More recently, whether police and the public are morally aligned (i.e., they share similar values) has been seen to be an additional and important element of police legitimacy (Jackson et al. 2012, 2013). So trust and confidence alone are not enough to capture the full definition of legitimacy. Trust, in addition to moral alignment and felt obligation to obey authorities, is an important aspect of police legitimacy.

So how do police obtain and maintain legitimacy? What can they do to encourage this perception among the policed public? Academic research consistently finds there are two key antecedents of police legitimacy. The first is the way people perceive police performance (Hinds and Murphy 2007; Sunshine and Tyler 2003). Police are expected to do their job well. It is unlikely that police will be perceived to be a legitimate authority if they lack the capacity to successfully undertake their core business, which is to prevent and control crime and disorder. The second antecedent is what Tyler and his colleagues term "procedural justice." Broadly speaking, PJ encapsulates the quality of police treatment of people and the quality of police decision making (Reisig et al. 2007; Sunshine and Tyler 2003; Tyler 2003). PJ in action can be broken down into four key elements or principles. These are: dignity and respect, trustworthy motives, neutrality, and voice. When police treat people with respect, demonstrate trustworthiness, are neutral in their decision making, and provide people with an opportunity to participate in the process and air concerns before decisions are made (i.e., voice), then people are more likely to believe police are being procedurally just (see also Goodman-Delahunty 2010; Sunshine and Tyler 2003; Tyler 2008; Tyler and Huo 2002). Research shows that while police performance is important to building a collective perspective of police legitimacy, it is the widespread use of PJ that is the most proximate and effective way to promote police legitimacy (Jackson et al. 2012; Murphy et al. 2008; Sunshine and Tyler 2003; for an exception, see Tankebe 2009a; Tyler and Fagan 2008). Thus, beyond the intrinsic value of treating people fairly, procedurally just policing can encourage widespread perceptions of police being legitimate (Tankebe 2009b, p. 8).

Ten Reasons Why PJ and Legitimacy Matter to Police

People Will Comply with the Law, Even When You Are Not Around

Most people intuitively know it is unlawful to attack another person, take property that belongs to someone else, or drive recklessly on the roads. Police are uniquely empowered to enforce laws and social norms to curb "self-interested individual behaviors that are destructive to society" (Tyler 2000, p. 983; see also Tyler 2001b). But according to Tyler (1990, 2006b) and others (see Jackson et al. 2012; Sunshine and Tyler 2003) compliance with police and the law is not explained solely by the threat of punishment or the use of coercive power. A sense that the police are legitimate can help explain why people comply with the law in the absence of a direct threat to their well-being and liberty. For example: Why do people obey traffic rules when the likelihood of apprehension is low? Tyler (2006a, p. 25) attributes this normative compulsion to obey the law to both an internalized sense of right and wrong and the "acceptance by people of the need to bring their behavior into line with the dictates of an external authority" (see also Easton 1958; Friedman 1975; Gerstein 1970). When people believe the police are legitimate, they are more willing to bring their behavior in line with the laws that the police represent (Tyler 1990, 2006b).

This argument stands up to empirical scrutiny. Sunshine and Tyler (2003) show a clear link between compliance with the law and the belief that police are legitimate (see also Jackson et al. 2012; Tyler 1990, 2006b; Tyler and Fagan 2008). In their US study, they asked survey participants how often they followed regulations about "where to park a car legally," "how to legally dispose of trash and litter," and "not making a noise at night" (Sunshine and Tyler 2003, p. 541). They also asked participants to rate the risk of "being caught and punished" for disregarding these regulations (Sunshine and Tyler 2003, p. 540). People were more likely to comply with the law if they viewed police as legitimate, while perceived risk of punishment played a less prominent role in predicting compliance. Sunshine and Tyler (2003) found PJ to be the key antecedent of people's perceptions of police legitimacy. Another example is the Paternoster et al. (1997) study. Using data collected in the *Milwaukee Domestic Violence Experiment*, they examined the link between PJ policing and the likelihood that offenders would reoffend. They found a lower rate of reoffending among domestic violence perpetrators when police were observed by the offenders to be using PJ (Paternoster et al. 1997).

These examples point to the ability of the police to encourage law-abiding behavior in the absence of direct police supervision. And police need citizens to comply with the law generally because most behavior takes place outside of police surveillance. The goal for police, therefore, is to get fewer people doing the wrong thing, fewer people who only do the right thing when the police are around, and more people doing the right thing when no one is around to catch any illegal behavior. Sounds simple enough?

People Will Comply with Police Directives

Maintaining law and order is the cornerstone of policing. But getting people to obey police directives is often fraught with difficulties. People argue with traffic police, yell abuses at police when police try to sort out domestic disturbances, hurl bottles and glasses at police when police move in to break up fights at parties, events, and sporting fixtures, and the list goes on. It is so much easier for police when people peacefully comply with directives. Getting people to do what you ask them to do, when you ask them to do it, is our second reason for suggesting why police should care about PJ and police legitimacy.

The research literature helps to explain the link between PJ, police legitimacy, and getting people to comply with police in face-to-face encounters. Clearly, police require citizens to comply with their requests and queries for information in order to do their job well (Mastrofski et al. 1996; McCluskey et al. 1999). Where compliance is not offered voluntarily, police officers can elicit compliance through coercive means. However, voluntary compliance may be more desirable because using force involves a degree of risk to the officer and citizen as well as other negative consequences (Schulhofer et al. 2011; Sunshine and Tyler 2003). Further, common sense tells us that arresting people for noncompliance has costs for the state and negative implications for the offender.

Observations of police–citizen encounters demonstrate that PJ is linked to compliance with police requests. For example, Mastrofski et al. (1996; see also McCluskey 2003; Mccluskey et al. 1999) observed police officers in their day-to-day activities. They took note of several police requests for compliance (e.g., that citizens: "…discontinue illegal behaviors," "leave another person alone or leave the premises," or "calm down or cease disorderly behavior"; Mastrofski et al. 1996,

p. 280). One of the key reasons for noncompliance was that citizens viewed the officer as disrespectful (recall that respect is an important component of PJ). This body of research, then, shows that when police treat people with dignity and respect, the encounter is less likely to escalate into a violent situation, it is more likely to reduce physical harm to both offenders and police, and it is more likely to garner greater levels of compliance with directives than when police demonstrate either verbally or nonverbally that they do not respect the citizens (see also Dai et al. 2011).

People Will Assist You

PJ and police legitimacy can also promote people's willingness to voluntarily cooperate with police. Citizen cooperation with police makes a difference to police effectiveness because citizens are the "eyes and ears" of the police (Sadd and Grinc 1994, p. 49). It is well known that citizens have a greater capacity to undertake informal surveillance compared to police. Hence, police rely on citizens to report crime and community problems and to assist police with their investigations (Tyler and Fagan 2008). Getting people to assist the police is the third reason why police care about police legitimacy and PJ.

Research shows that PJ and police legitimacy can encourage citizens' willingness to cooperate with police. For example, Sunshine and Tyler (2003, p. 541) found that PJ was the key antecedent of legitimacy, which, in turn, influenced people's willingness to call the police to report crime, accidents, and "dangerous or suspicious activities" as well as to provide police with information, and to engage in voluntary crime prevention activities (see also Tyler and Fagan 2008). Other research provides further support for this. Murphy et al. (2008) assessed citizens' perceptions of police before and after police ran a community policing program in an Australian suburb. They found that PJ and police legitimacy predicted "changes in cooperative behavior over time" (Murphy et al. 2008, p. 151).

Overall, the extant literature clearly shows that PJ policing has the potential to facilitate the role of citizens as agents of social control. In turn, information sharing and other cooperative behavior benefits the police, in that police are better equipped to prevent and control crime. We propose, therefore, that fostering police legitimacy is a very good way for police to garner help from citizens in the form of reporting incidents, undertaking crime prevention activities, and generally being helpful in the community.

People Will Be Satisfied with You

Satisfaction with police is measured across police jurisdictions all over the world. In our systematic search of police legitimacy (see S. Bennett et al. 2009), the measure of "satisfaction with police" was the most common outcome measured in studies assessing police legitimacy, as well as in those evaluating police interventions (see also Mazerolle et al. 2013b). Research consistently shows that procedurally just policing leaves citizens feeling more satisfied with a police encounter and can encourage acceptance of police decisions more so than in those encounters that do not use the key principles of PJ. Even when police are unable to deliver favorable outcomes to people (e.g., when a police officer issues a traffic ticket, the recipient is unlikely to view this as a favorable outcome), research shows that when police treat people in a procedurally just way they will be much more satisfied with the encounter and will be more willing to accept a decision. Making people satisfied with the police is therefore the fourth reason why PJ and police legitimacy matter to police.

We could list many studies that support the link between PJ, police legitimacy, and satisfaction with police. But we provide just a few here to illustrate our point. In an Australian study of 2,611 citizens, Hinds and Murphy (2007) found that people were more satisfied with police if they felt the police were legitimate. PJ was found to be the primary predictor of people's views of police legitimacy. In another study, Murphy (2009) reported findings from people who had had personal contact with police in the previous 12 months. Again, satisfaction with the police encounter was higher among those who believed police were more legitimate and procedurally just. In a US study, Tyler and Huo (2002) examined a sample of people who were stopped by police. Those who said they received PJ during the encounter were significantly more likely to accept a police officer's decision, regardless of the outcome of the encounter.

People are emotional beings (Murphy and Tyler 2008), and it is normal for them to react negatively to unfavorable outcomes. The studies above, however, suggest that treating people with PJ has the ability to increase acceptance of decisions and satisfaction with police, regardless of whether a decision was perceived as favorable. We propose, therefore, that the police have more to gain than to lose by engaging with people in a procedurally just way.

It Works with Some Vulnerable Groups

The studies cited so far present findings about police legitimacy and PJ from research conducted with general population samples. Research also shows, however, that PJ can be effective when applied within some (although not all) vulnerable groups in society. Police are generally the first port of call when citizens experience a distressing event such as becoming a victim of, or being a witness to, a crime. Studies show that if police use PJ in their encounters with most groups of vulnerable people, it leaves the vulnerable feeling more satisfied with the encounter. The exception is, perhaps, for those with cognitive impairment (see Chap. 6). But for other vulnerable groups—particularly those with a mental illness or those with recent experiences as a victim—PJ approaches by police result in better outcomes. For example, Elliott et al. (2011) interviewed 110 victims of crime about their encounters with police to ascertain what they most valued from police during interactions. They found that the PJ features of an encounter were just as important to victims as the police solving the crime. Similarly, in a study of 154 mentally ill people who had had a recent encounter with police, Watson et al. (2010) found that those who reported being treated with PJ felt less coerced by police, had a more positive emotional experience, had greater acceptance of decisions, and more strongly endorsed police as legitimate. Participants who felt police were procedurally just also reported lower levels of resistance and greater compliance with police. Reducing distress among vulnerable groups is the fifth reason why PJ and police legitimacy matter to police.

It Can Be Effective for Some Ethnic Minority Groups

Garnering support from ethnic minority groups is the sixth reason why police should care about police legitimacy and PJ. Policing ethnic minority groups poses specific challenges for police because minorities tend to be both less trusting of police and less likely to engage in collaborative crime control than nonminority groups (e.g., Cherney and Chui 2009; Skogan 2006). Research conducted in the UK and the USA has found that the underlying dynamics of the PJ effect are similar across different ethnic groups (see, for example, Bradford and Jackson 2010; Sunshine and Tyler 2003). While some groups are found to differ in their judgments about the quality of police treatment (e.g., African Americans tend to be more critical of police treatment than are White Americans; MacCoun 2005; Tyler and Huo 2002), these studies generally find PJ matters to minority groups for a range of outcomes, including perceptions of police legitimacy, and whether people would cooperate with police or seek their assistance (Bradford 2012; Sunshine and Tyler 2003; Tyler 2001a; Tyler et al. 2010). Because ethnic minority groups can present challenges to police, PJ may be an ideal tool to help improve relationships between police and ethnic minority groups.

Research explains these findings by saying that PJ and police legitimacy are important to those who may feel marginalized or uncertain about their place in society. It may be the most important first step that police can take toward building trust, garnering cooperation, eliciting compliance, and generally building rapport with otherwise disenfranchised groups of people in largely disadvantaged communities. However, these findings should be interpreted with some caution. New research indicates that PJ is not always the most important factor promoting police legitimacy among ethnic groups in particular contexts (Cherney and Murphy 2013; Murphy and Cherney 2011, 2012; Sargeant et al. in press). In particular, recent research in Australia shows that PJ and legitimacy, when used with ethnic minority groups, can sometimes be less effective than US or UK research suggests (Murphy and Cherney 2011, 2012; but see Murphy 2013). In Chap. 6, we discuss how police performance may be more important than PJ for some ethnic minority groups in society and how perceptions about the legitimacy of certain laws can interfere. For now, however, we suggest that police have a lot to gain by emphasizing PJ in their encounters with ethnic minorities, but that the use of PJ in these encounters should follow a considered approach, in light of the empirical evidence.

It is Easy, When You Get the Hang of It

While we recognize that PJ may be easier said than done, we contend that practicing PJ across a wide range of encounters will help institutionalize the delivery of PJ policing. The more you do it, the easier it will get! In this section, we highlight a few common police tactics that are easily adaptable to fostering legitimacy. As such, we argue that the seventh reason why police should do PJ in the context of their day-to-day activities is that the more it is done, the easier it gets.

The elements of PJ are well defined and are tried and tested across numerous contexts (e.g., occupational settings, legal settings, policing). GoodmanDelahunty (2010, p. 404) outlines the work of Tyler et al. (Tyler 2008; Tyler and Huo 2002; Tyler and Lind 1992), describing the elements of PJ as being four "key ingredients." These are "trustworthiness," "respectful treatment," "neutrality," and "voice" (Goodman-Delahunty 2010, p. 404; Tankebe 2009a). Trustworthiness can be demonstrated by caring about the "well-being" of citizens and acting in their "best interests" (Goodman-Delahunty 2010, p. 404). Respectful treatment involves a consideration for human rights, and treating people politely and with dignity (Goodman-Delahunty 2010; Tyler and Huo 2002). Neutrality and voice are about decision making: Police should be unbiased when making decisions, and they should allow citizens to "participate by expressing a viewpoint" (Goodman-Delahunty 2010, p. 405; Tyler 2008).

These key ingredients of PJ can be utilized by police during pretty much every type of policing activity. Braga and Weisburd (2010) describe a range of ways that police can incorporate PJ into a variety of policing tactics that focus on problem places. In the UK, the Metropolitan Police Service in London conducted a newsletter drop designed to increase public trust and confidence in the police (Hohl et al. 2010). The newsletter communicated to readers that police always try to act in citizens' best interests and encouraged citizens to express their views and contribute to police decision making. A subsequent evaluation of the newsletter drop suggested that confidence in police improved.

Mazerolle and her colleagues have also put PJ policing into practice in an experimental field trial (see Mazerolle et al. 2012, 2013a; Murphy et al. in press). The QCET—the focus of a large portion of this book—used PJ under randomized field trial conditions when police implemented alcohol breath testing operations with the public. Police either utilized a script that incorporated the principles of PJ, or used standard police practice. When evaluating this intervention, it was found that the experimental group was more satisfied with police and more willing to comply with the police officer during their encounter compared to the control group (although this effect was small, Mazerolle et al. 2012). Indeed, we cannot think of one single type of police intervention that cannot be modified, adapted, and implemented to explicitly incorporate the key ingredients of PJ (see also Chap. 2).

You Can Use PJ In-House

What goes around, comes around. The eighth reason why police should care about using PJ during encounters with the public is that we think that most police want to be treated in a dignified, trustworthy, and respectful way themselves. We suggest that in addition to facilitating positive outcomes with the general public, PJ is also a useful device within workplaces. PJ can aid with the acceptance of decisions made by superiors in workplace settings, as well as improve workplace satisfaction and commitment (Blader and Tyler 2003). In this way, police can incorporate the use of PJ not only when interacting with offenders, victims, witnesses, and the public at large, but also when interacting with other police officers (particularly when interacting with those lower in the chain of command).

A large number of studies support the use of PJ within organizations. For example, Cohen-Charash and Spector (2001, pp. 296–298) found that perceiving PJ in the workplace was associated with greater "pay satisfaction," "supervisor satisfaction," "management satisfaction," and "commitment to the organization." A lack of PJ was linked to "counterproductive work behaviors" (Cohen-Charash and Spector 2001, pp. 296–298). The relevance of PJ to workplaces has also been considered in research specifically about police. For example, Noblet et al. (2009) examined the link between PJ and officer stress and burnout. Through surveys with Australian police officers they found that "interpersonal fairness" (i.e., fairness demonstrated toward people within an organization) was linked to lower psychological distress (see also Noblet and Rodwell 2008; Noblet et al. 2009, p. 613). Incorporating the principles of PJ, therefore, into the day-to-day operations of policing can encourage better outcomes for police within their organization, including police compliance (see Bradford et al. 2013; Hogan and Stubbs 2003). We expand further on this notion of PJ within police organizations in Chap. 5.

You Will Be More Effective

The ninth reason why we think police should care about police legitimacy and PJ is that police will be more effective when they utilize the key ingredients of PJ policing than when they do not. Overwhelmingly, research indicates that PJ and legitimacy promote a willingness to obey police (see Jackson et al. 2012; Sunshine and Tyler 2003), compliance with the law (Jackson et al. 2012; Paternoster et al. 1997; Sunshine and Tyler 2003) and compliance with police officers (see Mastrofski et al. 1996), cooperation with police (see Beetham 1991; Murphy et al. 2008; Tyler and Fagan 2008), and satisfaction with police (see Hinds and Murphy 2007).

By using PJ, police will be better equipped to undertake their core business of preventing and controlling crime. They will also garner valuable assistance from the general public, including the most vulnerable groups in society. Thus, making the small changes required—using the elements of PJ (trustworthiness, respectful treatment, neutrality, and voice)—can help police and police agencies to be more effective. In other words, more PJ used in day-to-day activities helps to garner support from the general public, elicit cooperation and compliance, and makes people more satisfied. This in turn can lead police to be more effective in their crime control and prevention activities that in turn will make citizens believe that the police are doing a better job, which (in turn) can help police do an even better job of crime control.

Consistent Legitimate Practice Will Mean Less Force is Needed

Police have the authority to use force (i.e., weapons, restraints) and issue sanctions (i.e., fines, taking into custody) to gain obedience with the law. But why would police want to force people to obey the law if they do not have to? It is a lot of hard work that can be avoided if people universally respect the law and are willing to obey police authority in the absence of force. The key here is that people respect the law and obey police authority when they perceive the entire police agency to be legitimate. It is not enough for one individual officer to do the "right" thing if others in the agency do not. We offer, therefore, that the final reason why all police—and the police agency as a collective—should care about PJ and police legitimacy is that when police consistently use PJ in their encounters with citizens and are perceived to be legitimate, there is the potential for compliance with the law in the absence of force.

Summary

As we have noted above, generalized perceptions of police legitimacy lead to several positive outcomes for police: The public is more willing to comply with the law and with police, and cooperate and be more satisfied with police. Perhaps most importantly, as Mazerolle et al. (2013a) show, these generalized perceptions of police can be developed through very specific police use of PJ during encounters with the public. What the police do in each and every encounter matters (Mazerolle et al. 2013a; but see Skogan (2006) for an alternative view).

When citizens believe the police are legitimate, they are more willing to obey the police and are subsequently more willing to cooperate with the police and comply with the law in their everyday lives (Sunshine and Tyler 2003; Tyler 1990, 2006b). Legitimacy thus reflects the belief that an authority is entitled to the power that it wields and that the public has confidence in the ability of the authority to wield that power properly (see also Bottoms and Tankebe 2012; Jackson et al. 2012). Tom Tyler (1990, 2006b)—the leading scholar in this field—argues that people will often obey the police voluntarily when they believe that the police are legitimate.

Overall, we suggest police gain a lot when they are universally able to foster positive perceptions of legitimacy. While in Western societies (such as Australia and the USA) the vast majority of people will agree that the police are legitimate, there will be other societies that have less positive perceptions about police legitimacy. Individual officers can use the principles of PJ to encourage positive perceptions about legitimacy among individual citizens. However, in order to effect more global change, police need to work as a team and universally apply the key principles of PJ to produce generalized and positive views of police that then translate into a willingness of people to comply with the law. Easy? In a nutshell, it is up to all officers to do their bit for the good of the whole.

What Is to Follow

From the outset, we stated that this is a book about the "doing" of PJ. Our goal is to give police and scholars alike some ideas as to what the police might do to implement the principles of PJ. It is easy enough to say: Treat people with dignity and respect! Give citizens voice! Convey trustworthy motives! And be neutral! But, as with most things in life, putting ideas into practice is often easier said than done. Research from across the world shows that PJ can be done and is being done by police in places such as Australia (Mazerolle et al. 2013a; Murphy et al. 2008), the UK (Jackson et al. 2012), the USA (Tyler 1990, 2006b), and Israel (Coicaud 2002). We hope this book helps police to get on the PJ bandwagon and goes at least part of the way to demonstrating how it is—or could be—done.

In Chap. 2, we examine the practical ways that the police can approach engagement with citizens across a range of different types of interventions (problem-oriented policing, patrols, restorative justice, reassurance policing, community policing) in order to embrace the principles of PJ. In Chap. 3, we identify the outcomes of police interventions using PJ elements, and then in Chap. 4, we introduce the QCET, highlight the importance of procedurally just "dialog," and describe QCET dialog that specifically operationalized the key PJ constructs. In Chap. 5, we look into the black box of QCET to reveal the difficulties of trying to get PJ dialog into police encounters with citizens. Chapter 5 draws on interviews and survey responses from police who participated in QCET in order to identify the types of challenges that we experienced in getting police to engage with the dynamic PJ dialog. Moving to the broader context of QCET, in Chap. 6 we focus on the range of barriers that confronted the launch and implementation of QCET. This is not a chapter about the research challenges, but more about the organizational and operational challenges that confronted—and continue to confront—police leaders wanting to build PJ into daily practice. In our concluding chapter—Chap. 7—we discuss some of the barriers for implementing procedurally just ways of interacting with citizens and offer some insights for reform.

Chapter 2
Getting a Little More PJ in Your Day

Introduction

In Chap. 1, we demonstrated how important it is that the public believe that the police are legitimate, and we identified procedural justice (PJ) as the key antecedent of legitimacy. So, how can police improve public perceptions of legitimacy in their day-to-day activities? How do police get a little more PJ in their day? What types of police tactics and interventions lend themselves to the "doing" of PJ? Clearly, many different types of police tactics, interventions, and approaches could incorporate elements of PJ and could improve public perceptions of legitimacy, but what exactly might comprise PJ-enhancing strategies and interventions?

In the current chapter, we draw on an extensive collection of studies that were part of a systematic search (see Bennett et al. 2009) and review (see Mazerolle et al. 2013b) that described evaluations of interventions designed to build police legitimacy. In our reading of this literature, we identified a range of different policing interventions that have incorporated PJ and/or sought to improve legitimacy. We focus on ways that police might incorporate PJ into their day-to-day routine.

We begin by summarizing how we collected the police studies and then discuss how we categorized the interventions into four broad groups according to the typology put forth by Weisburd and Eck (2004). For each of the broad policing categories (community policing, problem-oriented policing, hot-spots policing, and the standard model of policing), we describe how these policing approaches can enhance legitimacy and how including and/or emphasizing elements of PJ can best achieve this goal.

Gathering the Studies

The systematic search (Bennett et al. 2009) and review (Mazerolle et al. 2013b) gathered studies from all over the world that explored and evaluated police-led interventions to enhance citizen perceptions of police legitimacy. Published and unpublished studies up until 2009 (an updated search and review is in the works) were

L. Mazerolle et al., *Procedural Justice and Legitimacy in Policing*,
SpringerBriefs in Criminology, DOI 10.1007/978-3-319-04543-6_2,

identified using six electronic databases (CSA, Informit, Ingenta Connect, Ovid, Proquest, and Web of Knowledge), two library catalogs (National Police Library and the Cambridge University Library and dependent libraries), reference lists of eligible studies, as well as the biographies and publication lists of authors influential in the field of PJ and legitimacy. Search keywords focused on terms relating to police legitimacy, PJ, and police effectiveness and resulted in over 20,000 relevant abstracts (see Bennett et al. 2009). Screening of these documents identified 963 unique studies incorporating police legitimacy and/or the elements of PJ policing including dignity and respect, trustworthy motives, neutrality, and citizen participation (i.e., voice). Of the 963 studies identified in the search, 163 contained empirical evaluations of police-led interventions (see Mazerolle et al. (2013b) for a complete list of studies).

In this chapter, we draw on studies identified through the systematic search that sought to improve police legitimacy, or interventions that included an element of PJ as a component of the outcome or intervention. Collectively, these studies help to illustrate the variety of ways that police might improve legitimacy, with a specific focus on how police might incorporate PJ into many different types of day-to-day policing strategies.

We have used Weisburd and Eck's (2004) four broad categories of policing intervention approaches to group the policing studies described in this chapter. These categories vary mostly in their focus and content (e.g., mostly law enforcement versus interventions using a variety of crime control partners). *Community policing* includes interventions that rely on strong police–community partnerships (including restorative justice (RJ) and school-based interventions) that utilize a diverse range of approaches to deal with a broad spectrum of crime problems. In contrast to community policing, *problem-oriented policing (POP)* interventions are highly focused on *specific* problems or people and involve police partnerships with other entities to reduce crime and disorder. *Hot-spots policing* involves law-enforcement-focused strategies (in contrast to POP, which involves a broader range of problem-solving approaches) aimed at problem people and/or places. Finally, the *standard model of policing* includes generalized, law enforcement responses without a focus on specific problem people or places. Using the four Weisburd–Eck categories to describe a range of police-led interventions, we highlight how police-led interventions can embrace PJ as part of the approach, infusing some of those "key ingredients" of PJ into their activities and show that there are many ways for police to get more PJ in their day, even within the existing range of police interventions.

Community Policing

Community policing strategies are naturally and easily oriented to incorporate the principles of PJ, offering an ideal vehicle for utilizing the principles of PJ to enhance police legitimacy in the community. The PJ elements of citizen voice (i.e., participation) and demonstrating trustworthy motives are particularly easily adapted to community policing interventions. Community policing involves the "coproduction" of community safety and the development of working relationships with the community (Greene 2000, p. 311). While community policing includes a broad range of principles and practices (Mastrofski 2006; and see the COPS website—www.cops.usdoj.gov—for improved tools to measure community policing components), there are commonalities across community policing approaches. These include police working in closer contact with communities, engaging in problem-solving activities, and mobilizing community residents to get involved in community regulation (Bayley 1994; Cordner 1998; Kelling and Moore 1988; Myhill 2006; Skogan 2006). This section of the chapter presents "general" models of community policing, "restorative justice" processes, and "school-based policing" to demonstrate the variety of programs and strategies that encompass community policing approaches for getting more PJ in your day.

General Models of Community Policing

The foundational elements of community policing are expected to enhance legitimacy outcomes, such as trust, satisfaction with police, and citizen cooperation. Table 2.1 presents a summary of general community policing studies identified through our research (e.g., see Mazerolle et al. 2013b) and we discuss each of these strategies below.

Weed and Seed: The Weed and Seed approach involves increasing police–community interactions to control violent and drug crime, and to respond to local community problems in targeted high-crime neighborhoods (Dunworth and Mills 1999a). The name of this approach is derived from an explicit goal to "weed" out offenders and disorder and "seed" initiatives to improve community capacity. Weed and Seed readily activates PJ elements, such as *trustworthy motives, dignity and respect,* and *citizen participation* when police "establish mutual trust between law enforcement and the public," "enlist the community's help in identifying patterns of criminal activity," and "enable residents in the target area to improve their community morale" (Dunworth and Mills 1999a, b, c, pp. 1–2). Weed and Seed programs also provide police with opportunities to participate in community events, such as school activities, which allow police informal settings to communicate with the public and enhance trust (see Dunworth and Mills 1999a, b, c). While all Weed and Seed operations do not automatically implement the four principles of PJ, they can provide a useful vehicle for police to communicate PJ to citizens.

Neighborhood Watch: Neighborhood watch programs enable citizens to play a pivotal role in local crime management and emergency preparedness. A group of citizens within a defined neighborhood work in partnership with police. While the specific activities may vary, citizens generally volunteer to assist with monitoring and report suspicious events to police, and police provide information about crime in the community and crime-prevention techniques. Neighborhood watch and similar community-based interventions offer police ideal opportunities to interact

Table 2.1 Community policing

Intervention name	Description of approaches
Weed and seed	Targeted policing in particular geographical locations to "weed" out offenders and disorder, and "seed" areas with explicit initiatives to strengthen community capacity
Neighborhood watch	Police–community partnership to discuss crime trends and prevention
Reassurance policing	Implementation of local schemes to ease fear of crime and rationalize perceptions of risk and safety
	Increase police presence, community involvement, and targeted policing initiatives
Beat policing	Dedicated police officer to certain geographical location to increase police–community relations
	Small police stations positioned in residential areas or shopping centers
Dedicated police teams	Police teams dedicated to crime detection and prevention in specific locations
Increased visibility	Increase police visibility and enhance approachability from public
Citizen contact patrols	Police officers offer crime-prevention programs
	Disseminate informative crime-prevention brochures to the public
Interagency collaboration	Police responsibility for follow-up on domestic violence calls increased communication and enhanced propensity to report crime
	Communication among relevant services and agencies to increase intelligence sharing and crime reduction
	Improved communication among police and the community to reduce prevalence of crime
	Prostitutes encouraged to report violent clients to outreach services that inform the police and other prostitutes

with residents and obtain their views about community problems and community safety. During community meetings, police can demonstrate that they are fair and equitable by explaining their reasons behind crime control and prevention priorities. Police can also encourage citizens to participate and "have voice" (in PJ terms), by making time during meetings for citizens to express their views. In addition, community forums provide police with a great opportunity to market police successes and strategies used to prevent/reduce crime, demonstrating that they are trustworthy representatives of the community and that they care about community problems (Jackson and Bradford 2009).

Reassurance Policing: Reassurance policing strategies involve the police working in collaboration with the community to specifically respond to community priorities and neighborhood problems. This policing approach gives community members the ability to voice their concerns and enables police to prioritize their response in order to maximize public satisfaction (Tuffin et al. 2006) and community safety (Singer 2004). When the public perceive that the police are listening *and* actively responding to their concerns, they are reassured that police are acting legitimately (Singer

2004). Reassurance policing is therefore a useful avenue to explore when police are seeking to improve police legitimacy and to incorporate the principles of PJ into their interactions with the public.

Beat Policing: Beat policing is a well-known community policing strategy. However, the traditional "bobby on the beat" role has expanded significantly in recent years. Officers who are responsible for a defined area or beat are expected to go beyond just foot patrols. Today, beat policing involves dedicated officers who liaise with local organizations to improve community areas, identify and respond to community problems, and attend community meetings. Bond and Gow's (1997) study of the beat policing program in Toowoomba, Qld, Australia, for example, assigned police officers to particular beats. These officers were wholly responsible for area foot patrols, answering calls for service, and solving problems within their beat so as to develop a positive rapport with local residents. Beat policing provides an opportunity for dedicated officers to get more PJ in their day when they provide citizens with opportunities to discuss and respond to concerns, and these officers are neutral in their decision making and promote solutions in these everyday encounters.

Dedicated Police Teams: Dedicated police teams aim to develop, cultivate, and deepen key relationships with community stakeholders around a dedicated area and/or problem (e.g., problematic housing estate). Dedicated teams are not normally redirected to other work and therefore provide the community with continuity when the same police rotate on and off shifts in the same geographic areas. In a study conducted in West Yorkshire, Brownlee and Walker (1998) found that the dedicated police teams established wide-ranging networks with individuals and groups within schools, neighborhood watches, and community forums and were able to foster community cooperation because of the time police spent with key individuals/groups in engaging ways (e.g., litter clear-ups, community sporting events). Dedicated teams can encourage citizen participation and further optimize PJ when they foster trustworthy relationships within the community.

Increased Visibility: Our review identified PJ ingredients in a range of approaches aimed at increasing police visibility, such as foot patrols (Holmberg 2005; Pate and Annan 1989), mini police stations (Moon et al. 2005), and police shop fronts (Taylor and Charlton 2005). We have included the increased visibility studies under the banner of "community policing" (rather than the standard model of policing), because in these studies the police engaged in activities that made them more accessible to the public and used PJ elements as part of this process. For example, in 1992, the Queensland Police Service implemented a shop front program which resulted in 49 small police offices in shopping centers and central business districts in Queensland (Taylor and Charlton 2005). Shop front police beat officers built relationships with retailers when they listened to their concerns, provided retailers with valuable information about crime and safety tips, encouraged them to report crime, and were accessible when retailers did need to a report crime (Taylor and Charlton 2005). The authors unsurprisingly found that retailers who had a police shop front were significantly more likely to report crime than retailers who did not. Police can maximize the benefits of such encounters by making sure that all such encounters are packed with PJ.

Citizen Contact Patrols: The citizen contact patrol strategies involve developing and maintaining contact with residents and informing them of crime-prevention techniques. T. Bennett (1990) found that consistent police contact with residents—including door-knocking, a persistent policing presence in the community, and identifying and responding to citizen concerns—fostered greater trust in police. Beedle (1984) found that a citizen contact patrol initiative (police provided information on burglary prevention and detection techniques) yielded similar results. Citizen contact patrols provide opportunities for police to get more PJ into their encounters, particularly around eliciting citizen participation (i.e., giving citizens "voice") in setting priorities and developing solutions to neighborhood crime problems.

Interagency Collaboration: Interagency collaboration represents another opportunity for police to include more PJ within the community policing context. Interagency collaboration refers to interventions where police actively use formal arrangements with other organizations to address a wide array of crime problems and/or to improve service delivery. When there is a high degree of common purpose, collaborative relationships between police and other organizations can greatly assist in increasing or improving the effectiveness of a jointly supported or undertaken enterprise.

When police portray trustworthy motives and actively involve and engage other organizations in deciding how to solve problems, it allows them to collaborate effectively with a range of organizations and groups when tackling numerous policing problems. In addition, police can maximize the benefits and/or responses to specific problems by including relevant agencies with specialty skills. For example, Davis and Taylor (1997) explored an interagency response to repeat domestic violence victims. Police enlisted the support of social workers and education for follow-up appointments with victims and their perpetrators (if present). A dialog between victims and specialists provided an opportunity for participants to learn about the legal, personal, and social nature of domestic violence and receive referrals or on-the-spot counseling where required. This joint response increased participants' confidence in the ability of *police* to handle domestic violence *even though* the police were not responsible for the delivery of the whole intervention (e.g., social workers conducted the counseling and/or referrals).

Overall, interagency collaboration provides an important avenue for police to foster legitimacy. While police could arguably engage in these strategies in a transactional way, these strategies point to opportunities for police to incorporate PJ into their interactions not only with citizens, but also with organizations. Police can also improve performance by showing leadership and problem-solving skills. As Matthews (1993) suggests: strong and coordinated collaboration is dependent on shared priorities and commitments, resources, responsibility and accountability, as well as formalized protocols that can be maintained when shifts in leadership occur.

Restorative Justice Processes

Restorative processes are being increasingly incorporated within courts (e.g., diversion), police stations (e.g., cautions), prisons (e.g., adjudications), and schools (e.g., bullying interventions) to reduce, resolve, or prevent harmful behavior from occurring (Sherman and Strang 2007; Wenzel et al. 2008). While there are many different approaches that use restorative processes—such as mediation, family group conferences, RJ conferences, and court-ordered restitution—the underlying aim is to empower parties with a stake in a specific problem to collectively resolve how the problem should be dealt with (see Marshall 1999). As such, they are an example of community policing. RJ processes linked to policing generally include:

1. A respectful process that involves deliberative dialog assisted by a neutral facilitator/convenor
2. Disapproval of the offending and/or noncompliant behavior
3. An understanding and acknowledgment of how people have been affected
4. A plan put in place that allows affected parties to move forward
5. The capacity to follow-through to escalate regulatory intervention in the face of continuing noncompliance (in some RJ approaches)

PJ ingredients (neutrality, voice, dignity and respect, and trustworthy motives) are foundational within each of these RJ components. Consequently, it is not surprising that RJ approaches share with PJ the goal of developing informal and formal *legal procedures* that strengthen the influence of social values on law-abiding behavior. When dealing with people who have broken social rules, the aim of RJ "...should be to seek ways to heighten the future motivations that those people have to engage psychologically and behaviorally in society" (Tyler 2006a, p. 315). Tyler (2006a, p. 315) argues, therefore, that this engagement "...includes developing or becoming more committed to social values that promote self-regulation, and consequently adhering more closely to laws and social regulations in the future." RJ aims to facilitate and enhance self-regulatory actions by encouraging feelings of remorse in the offender, along with an acceptance of responsibility for actions and a connectedness to family, friends, and community. The idea is that this commitment, in turn, works against future transgressions of the law (Braithwaite 2002).

When people develop greater feelings of responsibility to others in the community, they become more motivated to either follow their moral principles or obey social authorities or institutions. Some evidence also suggests that RJ conferences build internal motivation to defer to authority in the future (Tyler 2006a). RJ processes often involve third parties, such as regulatory agencies and other services (see Mazerolle and Ransley 2005). These agencies and services help provide the participants with an understanding of the legal consequences of the issue at hand and offer direct access to a range of support services and resources.

Most evaluations of RJ report face-to-face meetings between affected parties, supporters, and support agencies. Although conferences can be convened by a civilian, when police endorse, facilitate, and/or support RJ, improved perceptions of

Table 2.2 Restorative processes

Intervention name	Description of approaches
Restorative cautioning	Use of RJ-based script for police to use to caution offenders and promote deterrence
Restorative justice conferencing	Police facilitation of family conference meeting to aid interaction between juvenile offender and their family to discuss implications of harm caused and appropriate reparations
Police-led mediation	Police assist in mediation process to aid dispute resolution processes

police legitimacy can result. Police also have direct power to enforce the outcomes of the conference (Moore and O'Connell 1994).

Our systematic review identified restorative processes which incorporated at least one of the PJ principles and evaluated the impact of the intervention on legitimacy outcomes, such as citizens' confidence in police, satisfaction with police, and perceptions about PJ (see also Chap. 3). Table 2.2 presents a summary of these processes (see Mazerolle et al. 2013b), which include restorative cautioning, police facilitated conferences, and police-led mediation. We discuss each of these interventions below.

Restorative Cautioning: Restorative cautioning uses a structured PJ dialog during a formal police disposal. Hoyle et al. (2002) found that police facilitated interactions to address the offense and its consequences in a neutral and respectful manner. This involved police using a script that emphasized neutrality throughout the process and stressed the importance of giving each individual voice at each stage of the encounter with the offender.

Restorative Conferencing: The studies that described the PJ elements of restorative conferencing (see McCold 2003; McCold and Wachtel 1998; Shapland et al. 2008; Sherman et al. 1998) found that the key way police used PJ was by facilitating impartial discussion (Shapland et al. 2006; Sherman et al. 1998) and voluntary participation (McCold 2003), ensuring that respect was given to all parties when discussing the harms caused by offenses (Shapland et al. 2008) and reaching an agreement that enhanced both victim and offender satisfaction (McCold and Wachtel 1998).

Police-Led Mediation: In police-led mediation, police act as a third party, resolving disputes between victims and offenders. Officers are trained in mediation (Volpe and Phillips 2003) and subsequently ensure that each party maintains mutual respect and participates voluntarily in the resolution process. If police act as a neutral third party in such encounters, one would expect that perceptions of PJ and police legitimacy would improve.

Table 2.3 School-based policing

Intervention name	Description of approaches
Informal contact	Integration of police officers into school-based activities to enhance communication and trust in police
Gang resistance education and training	School-based program led by police officers to educate and inform students against gang formation and criminality
Truant recovery program	Cooperative intervention by police and school personnel to reduce incidence of truancy and increase identification of at-risk students
School resource officers	Dedicated police officers provide services including counseling and crime-prevention information and education to reduce onset of criminality

School-Based Policing

We present the school-based policing interventions identified in our review under the broad umbrella of "community policing." School-based officers are typically embedded within schools in order to promote positive relationships between the police and the school community and to encourage a safe learning environment. These types of initiatives allow officers to take part in the day-to-day activities of the school (Dogutas 2007; Murray 2003), or they may involve more short-term programs where police officers visit schools either for targeted talks (Sellers et al. 1998) or to deliver certain programs (e.g., to combat truancy, see White et al. 2001). School-based policing initiatives allow the school-based police officers to interact with students and teachers, counsel students at risk of offending, and educate students on the law and the role of police in society. Some officers get involved in a variety of activities within the school, including helping teachers to develop curricula on law and police duties, engaging in partnerships with other agencies regarding youth welfare, and providing advice regarding personal safety and crime prevention. They are also able to attend to police-related matters within the school community.

The school-based community policing strategies in our pool of eligible studies include informal contact, gang resistance education, truancy programs, and school resource officers. All school-based interventions aimed to enhance students' trust and confidence in police through the implementation of a range of informal integrative initiatives and educational training sessions to aid interaction and mutual cooperation. Table 2.3 presents a summary of the approaches, each of which we discuss below.

Informal Contact: Informal contact studies promote informal interactions between police and schoolchildren in nonconfrontational situations. In her study, for example, Hinds (2009) describes that police used PJ by being fair and neutral in all interactions with adolescents and had a clear intent to enhance young people's perceptions of police (Hinds 2009). Informal contact is one way that police can engage in positive interactions with school children and incorporate PJ principles.

Gang Resistance Education: Gang resistance approaches involve police visiting schools and giving talks on conflict resolution and ways that young people can resist gang recruitment (Sellers et al. 1998; Winfree et al. 1999). The key aim of these programs is to convey factual information in a nonjudgmental (e.g., neutral decision making) and professional manner with nonpersonal examples (dignity and respect), provide information and alternatives to gang involvement (trustworthy motives), and engage people in discussion (citizen participation). When PJ ingredients are activated, these programs provide an opportunity for young people to perceive the police as legitimate.

Truancy Programs: Truancy reduction approaches involve police facilitating discussions between the truanting child, his or her parent, teachers, and other relevant services. In a study evaluated by White and colleagues (2001), the police allowed the child to voluntarily voice his or her issues and provided a forum for all parties to develop a deeper, more nuanced understanding of the factors contributing to the child's truancy. By allowing children to have a voice (one element of PJ) in these types of interactions, police have the potential to improve perceptions of police legitimacy.

School Resource Officers: PJ in this context is integrated into education and counseling programs by school resource officers (Dogutas 2007; Murray 2003). The role of school-based resource officers (see evaluations by Dogutas 2007 and Murray 2003) is to develop rapport with students, treat students with respect, and promote trustworthy motives by representing themselves as people students can confide in and approach if or when they were experiencing difficulties in their lives (Murray 2003). Again, creating a positive forum for police–citizen interactions is conducive to the implementation of PJ principles.

Problem-Oriented Policing

Like community policing, problem-oriented policing (POP) requires police to look beyond traditional policing strategies and develop a wide array of solutions to problems. In contrast to community policing, POP interventions are highly focused, either on problem places or on problem people. POP is also distinguished from the standard model and hot-spots policing through its use of a "diversity of approaches" (Weisburd and Eck 2004, p. 45). Herman Goldstein originally conceptualized POP in the late 1970s in order to address the focus in police agencies on responding to crime incidents (Goldstein 1990). Rather than simply reacting to violations of the law, POP shifts "the prime focus of the police away from incidents toward identifying, understanding, and solving problems" (Reisig 2010, p. 2). The process of solving problems involves police working with citizens and other crime control partners

Table 2.4 Problem-oriented policing

Intervention name	Description of approaches
Problem solving Policing generally	Data-driven initiatives to identify crime-prone areas and citizens Implementation of targeted enforcement strategies to reduce and prevent crime
Traffic safety enforcement	Concentrated enforcement of traffic laws to reduce casualties and enhance compliance with road rules
Drug enforcement	Targeted enforcement to reduce underage drinking through intercepting fake ID use
Vehicle theft reduction	Improved compliance regulation through vehicle certification labels to better identify stolen vehicles
Firearms initiative	Identification of problem areas and increased patrols and rapid intervention
Domestic violence initiatives	Implementation of alarm system for at-risk families of domestic violence to deter potential perpetrators and enable police to be informed and attend any potential incidents
Juvenile crime prevention	Identification of risk and protective factors among juveniles to reduce criminality by geographic location Police enforcement of juvenile curfew through arrests and deterrence
Homicide and violence reduction partnership	Data-driven strategy to identify problem and tailor solution, with a feedback component to revise and improve strategies
Environment-based crime prevention	Geographically based crime reduction strategy involving cooperation between police and business owners and modifications to infrastructure to reduce incidence of crime

to identify problems, implement solutions, and analyze the results (Scott and Kirby 2012). During the problem-solving process, POP provides opportunities for police to interact and work with the communities they serve and to demonstrate improved effectiveness (see also Braga and Weisburd 2010). POP is therefore one vehicle that can be used to improve police legitimacy by engaging with the community, using PJ. Table 2.4 summarizes a number of POP approaches identified in our review (see Mazerolle et al. 2013b)

As Table 2.4 illustrates, POP approaches are focused on specific crime problems and can be adapted to a wide range of issues, such as general crime prevention/reduction, traffic law enforcement, drug law enforcement, vehicle theft reduction, firearms, domestic violence, juvenile crime, homicide, and environment-based crime prevention. Because of the highly focused nature of these interventions, this section will not go into detail on each intervention strategy. Rather, what we wish to convey is that PJ can be promoted within a range of different types of POP approaches that target a wide range of problems.

While POP strategies do not, as a rule, have to incorporate PJ, there is a wide range of ways that police can infuse PJ into their POP activities. The Indianapolis Violence Reduction Program, evaluated by McGarrell and Chermak (2004a), for example, aimed to reduce violence through a number of activities including advertisements about the dangers of violent crime, increased police patrols, and meetings with those at risk. The program was designed to communicate a critical trustworthy motive that violent crime "...would not be tolerated in Indianapolis and surrounding communities" (McGarrell and Chermak 2004a, p. 148). Most important, at least for understanding how PJ can be incorporated into POP, was how the authors noted that "relationship building" was central to the program's success (McGarrell and Chermak 2004a). In this example, the police built relationships with "neighborhood leaders, faith-based community leaders and service providers" by providing opportunities for these stakeholders to have a voice in identifying issues and solutions. While not explicitly stated, it is expected that police treated these stakeholders with dignity and respect when implementing the program, which, they suggest, helped police to build legitimacy in the community (McGarrell and Chermak 2004a, p. 217).

Hot-Spots Policing

Hot-spots policing involves directed police patrols, yet it is different from the standard model of policing due to the higher "level of focus" on problem people and places (Weisburd and Eck 2004, p. 45). The idea of concentrating law enforcement resources on particular geographic locations emerges from the body of research showing that a large proportion of crime is attributable to a small number of geographic locations (Braga and Weisburd 2010; Sherman et al. 1989; Weisburd et al. 1992). Police expect that by increasing levels of enforcement focus to these crime-prone areas, they will be more effective in terms of crime control (Braga 2005; Braga and Weisburd 2010; Weisburd and Eck 2004).

Our review of the extant literature identified just three hot-spots studies, to date, that measured legitimacy as an *outcome* (Goldkamp and Vilcica 2008; Novak et al. 1999; Weisburd et al. 2011). These studies evaluated the use of geographically focused police crackdowns: one that aimed to reduce the incidence of disorder crimes in response to community concerns (Novak et al. 1999), one that focused on reducing burglaries through increased police presence and aggressive policing of citizens (Goldkamp and Vilcica 2008), and the other (Weisburd et al. 2011) that examined the impact of broken windows policing at crime hot spots on fear of crime, ratings of police legitimacy, and reports of collective efficacy among residents of targeted hot spots. While engaging in procedurally just interactions with citizens is not necessarily the goal of hot-spots policing, police spending time in hot spots offers many opportunities for police to improve trust and satisfaction in police (Braga and Weisburd 2010). For example, if police officers were to simply greet local business owners and community residents, explain why increased patrols were taking place, and perhaps ask for help and information, police could demonstrate that they care

Table 2.5 Standard enforcement model of policing

Intervention name	Description of approaches
Violence response teams	Provided with skills to address specific violent crime occurrences (e.g., DV) to reduce severity of harm and propensity for repeat victimization
Organized crime team response	Use of focused cross-agency collaborative efforts assisted in better identifying organized crime
Victim assistance and child protection teams	Coordinated police and volunteer crisis team with central purpose to reduce repeat victimization by educating, encouraging and validating victims, and providing personal follow-up if needed
	Specialized and effective police/agency structure resulting from improvements to quality of communication, decision making, openness and honesty of working relationships
Traffic enforcement teams	High visibility traffic team with focus on intercepting and stopping vehicles of interest. In this approach, legitimacy is an *outcome* of police effectiveness; however, police can pack PJ into these approaches during police–driver interaction
	Officers use PJ ingredients in their high volume and short encounter with drivers during random breath testing (RBT)
Police response teams	Collaboration among multiple community organizations and police to address family violence

about the community and its problems and thereby use their hot-spots patrols to build legitimacy.

Standard Enforcement Model of Policing

The standard model of policing is an enforcement approach that focuses on one-size-fits-all law enforcement activities, primarily in the form of reactive patrol strategies that seek to suppress crime (Weisburd and Eck 2004). Day-to-day enforcement is clearly the key area where police can apply PJ. The model generally involves unfocused preventive patrols, traffic officers enforcing speed zones, or officers responding to a myriad of calls for police service. During these kinds of law enforcement activities, police are often required to follow standard operating procedures (SOP) and specifically defined protocols. Table 2.5 presents a summary of standard enforcement approaches drawn from our collection of studies.

The standard enforcement model of policing category includes a wide array of traditional, unfocused, diffused law enforcement strategies, and specialized policing teams or taskforces that mostly measure the impact of the interventions on perceptions of police legitimacy (e.g., the outcome). Standard models of enforcement, however, represent a fundamental "bread and butter" opportunity for police to infuse PJ in day-to-day interactions with victims (e.g., domestic violence), offenders (e.g., traffic infringements), and support agencies.

Standard enforcement approaches from our collection of studies included child protection activities (Lardner 1992), rapid response to family violence (Lardner 1992), street-level policing around mental health problems (Tennant 1986), investigations in homicide cases (Schmitz et al. 1998), disorder policing (Rubenser 2000), street-level drug law enforcement (Battle 1999), policing gang violence (Katz 1997), and traffic enforcement (Henderson et al. 2004; Mazerolle et al. 2012). Tennant (1986), Turnbull et al. (1996), and Lardner (1992), for example, found that proactive interventions undertaken by a specialized police unit, working in collaboration with health and social services personnel, reduced recidivism rates. PJ techniques included police officers identifying and responding to individuals' immediate and long-standing crises using active listening skills, assertiveness, and sensitivity (citizen voice and participation). At the same time, the police demonstrated trustworthy motives and neutrality when they ensured that perpetrators had access to appropriate resources and social services and used networks of social service providers to provide stable support systems for the individuals (see Tennant 1986; Turnbull et al. 1996). Our search also found that collaborative and focused responses—those combining the expertise of both police and civil service agencies—are promising for garnering voluntary cooperation and satisfaction from both victims and offenders (Battle 1999; Schmitz et al. 1998). Random breath testing (RBT) is an example of a standard enforcement approach which can use all of the ingredients of PJ. In the Queensland Community Engagement Trial (QCET; Mazerolle et al. 2012), police used a PJ-scripted dialog with drivers. More detail on QCET is provided throughout this book but is highlighted here to emphasize that routine standard enforcement approaches can easily be made into opportunities for police to get more PJ in their day.

Summary Comments

This chapter highlighted some of the practical ways in which police officers have implemented and can implement the principles of PJ to enhance citizen perceptions of legitimacy across a wide range of different types of police activities. We used a body of studies gathered from a systematic search (see S. Bennett et al. 2009) and review (see Mazerolle et al. 2013b) to extract a wide range of policing strategies that aimed to improve legitimacy by utilizing PJ elements or approaches. The chapter highlights the applicability of PJ in a variety of policing contexts. We suggest, therefore, that the actual vehicle used in policing—the type of intervention—is not as important for fostering legitimacy as the substantive content of the interactions themselves. Getting more PJ into police work is, we show, possible across a wide range of different modes of police service delivery. But police do not need to implement a special tactic or strategy to implement PJ: Simply making day-to-day interactions with the public respectful is a great place to start.

Chapter 3
Outcomes of PJ Policing

Introduction

In Chap. 2, we explored the range of different ways police can get a little more procedural justice (PJ) into their various modes of service delivery. The studies presented in Chap. 2 provide many ideas for policing with more PJ across a wide range of interventions. Yet, the body of literature is limited in two significant ways: First, we do not know whether one element of PJ—voice, dignity and respect, trustworthy motives, or neutrality—is more important than another. And second, we have limited evidence about the relative differences across interventions in terms of building or influencing legitimacy-related outcomes. In this chapter, we compare and contrast the different *outcomes* for the studies that claimed (either explicitly or implicitly) that they used PJ and/or that aimed to improve police legitimacy. All of these studies measured the impact of the intervention on citizen perceptions of police. Using the results of the systematic review (see Mazerolle et al. 2013b), we can stretch (perhaps) to say that there are some interesting, albeit subtle, variations in the way citizens perceive the police depending on the type of intervention used. Like Chap. 2, we use the heuristic of Weisburd and Eck's (2004) typology to assess the relative differences in reported outcomes. We recognize, from the outset, that these results are patchy: We do not have consistent data on all of the different modes of policing to be able to say, for example, whether problem-oriented policing (POP) is more likely to generate more favorable views of police relative to say, community policing or hot spots policing interventions. But this chapter is a starting point.

Outcomes of PJ in Community Policing

Our systematic review identified 38 general community policing interventions that explicitly described at least one PJ element as being part of the intervention and included direct legitimacy-related outcomes such as citizen perceptions of their willingness to cooperate or comply with police, perceptions of PJ, as well as perceptions of citizen satisfaction with police (Mazerolle et al. 2013b). In some of

L. Mazerolle et al., *Procedural Justice and Legitimacy in Policing*,
SpringerBriefs in Criminology, DOI 10.1007/978-3-319-04543-6_3,

Table 3.1 Community policing: summary of outcomes

	Number of effect sizes	Number of effect sizes with positive effects	% of studies with positive effect sizes
All direct outcomes	*36*	*32*	*88.9*
Legitimacy	2	1	50.0
Procedural justice	8	7	87.5
Compliance/cooperation	4	3	75.0
Satisfaction/confidence	22	21	95.5
All indirect outcomes crime	*15*	*13*	*86.7*

the studies, we were able to assess the impact of the interventions not only on legitimacy outcomes but also on crime rates. We identify the legitimacy-enhancing outcomes as "direct outcomes" and the crime rate outcomes as "indirect outcomes."

Meta-analysis is a statistical method for summarizing the results of a group of empirical studies. The approach "…focuses on the aggregation and comparison of findings of different research studies" (Lipsey and Wilson 2001, p. 2). Table 3.1 summarizes the results of the meta-analysis by categorizing the different types of outcomes measured (both the direct and the indirect outcomes) across the population of studies in the systematic review (column 1), tabulating the total number of effect sizes that were calculated in the systematic review (column 2), calculating the total number that were in a positive direction (column 3), and providing the percentage of studies with positive effect sizes (column 4). Effect sizes described in this chapter—and more generally in meta-analysis results—are used to quantify the differences between two groups. If there is a large difference between two groups, this will result in a large effect size. In this chapter, a positive effect occurs when the intervention group (the group that included PJ or legitimacy-related elements) shows a more positive result on the outcome being measured than the comparison group. Using these effect sizes, we can compare and contrast the relative strength of each outcome with at least a little bit of precision. The way we present each table in this chapter follows the same column layout and format as presented in Table 3.1.

As Table 3.1 shows, 36 community policing studies included in the Mazerolle and colleagues (2013) systematic review reported direct outcomes and 15 reported indirect outcomes. Overall, in terms of the direct, legitimacy-enhancing outcomes, 32 of the 36 effect sizes (88.9 %) reported positive outcome effects, showing that the overwhelming majority of PJ-enhancing interventions in the category of "Community Policing" generated legitimacy-enhancing outcomes. We calculated 22 effect sizes with outcomes of satisfaction and/or confidence, of which 95.5 % were positive. Clearly, of all the community policing effect sizes identified in the review, satisfaction and confidence in the police were the most commonly identified positive outcomes. Table 3.1 also shows that 15 effect sizes reported changes in crime as an indirect outcome, with 86.7 % of these indicating positive effects (i.e., a reduction in crime). This shows that police can reduce crime and also enhance citizen satisfaction with police and confidence in police, as well as improve people's overall sense of police legitimacy by simply including at least one PJ element within the context of their community policing interventions.

Table 3.2 Restorative processes: summary of direct and indirect outcomes

	Number of effect sizes	Number of effect sizes with positive effect	% of studies with positive effect sizes
All direct outcomes	*16*	*15*	*93.8*
Legitimacy	4	4	100.0
Procedural justice	5	5	100.0
Compliance/cooperation	4	4	100.0
Satisfaction/confidence	3	2	66.7
All indirect outcomes crime	*8*	*6*	*75*

The take-home message is that community policing is a useful vehicle for police to use the principles of PJ, particularly because it is a relatively easy medium in which to use the key principles: treating people with dignity and respect, giving voice to citizens during community policing encounters, treating people in a neutral way, and/or conveying trustworthy motives. Our meta-analysis also shows that nearly nine out of ten times (88.9 %), interventions that use PJ within the context of the interventions identified in Chap. 2 (such as Weed and Seed programs, neighborhood watch, beat patrols, and high-visibility activities) are going to have a positive effect on how people view the police.

Outcomes of PJ in RJ Conferencing

Six police-led mediation interventions provided sufficient statistical data to be included in our (Mazerolle et al. 2013b) systematic review. Table 3.2 summarizes the outcome of the meta-analysis where studies could contribute more than one outcome and follows the same format as in the previous section.

As Table 3.2 shows, police-led restorative justice (RJ) interventions had a positive impact on the way victims and offenders perceived the police. More than 90 % (93.8 %) of the studies show that conference participants felt that they were treated with dignity and respect, had an opportunity to have their say, and subsequently reported greater perceptions of police legitimacy than those that were not part of the conference intervention. Of all the RJ studies identified in the systematic review, 16 effect sizes measuring direct outcomes were examined, the most frequent being perceptions of PJ. For 15 of these 16 outcomes (93.8 %), the effect sizes were positive, meaning that the RJ interventions generated positive perceptions about police. People reported that the RJ interventions were procedurally just, such that they were more likely to comply and cooperate with police and that they were more satisfied and confident with police.

Table 3.2 also shows that eight of the RJ studies measured the impact of the intervention on crime. Of these eight studies, six (75 %) reported positive effect sizes, meaning a reduction in crime (measured as reoffending) as a result of the police using PJ within the context of the RJ intervention. These results mean that three-quarters of RJ-conferenced offenders—when police followed the principles of PJ—were less likely to re-offend compared to court-processed offenders. These results show that PJ used in the context of RJ conferencing can provide enormous benefits to police: It can lead to more positive perceptions of police and a reduction in re-offending.

The vehicle of conferencing is gaining a great deal of attention as a way to deal with young people in low-risk situations immediately on-site. While (as yet) untested, some policing districts in the UK have trained their officers to use "Street RJ": This is where police use the same "script" when responding to minor offenses (such as shoplifting) as that used in a larger, more formal, conference. Officers convene a very short conference on the spot between the offender admitting guilt, and the victim and parents (when the perpetrator is underage). Because of the immediacy of the response, this intervention is likely to have a greater impact on behavior than a delayed court-based response.

Outcomes of PJ in School-Based Policing

Only one of the school-based studies described in Chap. 2 provided sufficient data to be included in the final meta-analysis (see Mazerolle et al. 2013b). Qualitatively, however, we found that when police officers were involved in targeting a specific issue (typically truancy), school-based policing programs showed positive effects in terms of improving the behavior and academic achievements of students within the program. We did not find, however, any impact of the school-based interventions on measures of police contact with young people (as measured by street checks, arrests, and via incident reports). Likewise, we did not find evidence to show that these school-based programs changed students' perceptions of legitimacy of the police.

We note that school-based programs are typically placed in schools with a high level of truancy. The causal effect, however, of the placement of school-based officers in high-level truanting schools is not generally explored in the literature. It seems plausible that schools whose students have problem behaviors in the first instance would be more likely to be assigned a school-based officer. In programs where a police officer is embedded in the school community, students are able to interact with police in a routine manner. Overall, while there is evidence that youth who are engaged with police in positive ways perceive police as more legitimate (Hinds 2009), there is little evidence from these intervention studies to test this relationship.

Outcomes of PJ in Problem-Oriented Policing

Of the 24 POP studies identified in the systematic search (see Chap. 2), 5 POP studies explicitly described at least one PJ element as being part of the intervention and included data suitable for assessing the specific impact of these interventions

Table 3.3 Problem-oriented policing: summary of outcomes

	Number of effect sizes	Number of effect sizes with positive effect	% of studies with positive effect sizes
All direct outcomes	*2*	*2*	*100*
Legitimacy	–	–	–
Procedural justice	1	1	100
Compliance/cooperation	–	–	–
Satisfaction/confidence	1	1	100
All indirect outcomes crime	*3*	*1*	*33.3*

on direct outcomes including citizen perceptions of their willingness to cooperate or comply with police, perceptions of procedural justice, as well as perceptions of citizen satisfaction with police. Three studies also examined the impact of POP—undertaken using at least one of the ingredients of PJ—on crime. Table 3.3 summarizes the outcome of our meta-analysis (see Mazerolle et al. (2013b) for more details) using the format that is described for these summary tables earlier in the chapter.

As Table 3.3 shows, two studies (McGarrell and Chermak 2004a; Weisburd et al. 2008) identified outcomes from the interventions that specifically focused on PJ and satisfaction/confidence in police. Both of these studies showed that the POP intervention, which was described as including a PJ element, could enhance perceptions of satisfaction with police and people's perceptions that they thought the police were procedurally fair.

Table 3.3 also shows that three of the POP studies (see Hartstone and Richetelli 2003; McGarrell and Chermak 2004b; Weisburd et al. 2008) identified a measure of crime as an outcome. Only one of these POP studies (Hartstone and Richetelli 2005) showed a positive outcome (i.e., a reduction in crime). The lack of studies that assess the impact of POP on perceptions of police legitimacy might mean one of three things:

1. POP is a weak vehicle for building legitimacy (not likely).
2. There is a systemic failure of POP evaluations to define or articulate POP interventions as incorporating the key elements of PJ, even if they do include these principles during POP interventions (highly likely).
3. There are many missed opportunities for fostering legitimacy within the context of POP (likely).

The basic POP paradigm in policing provides an ideal vehicle for police to foster legitimacy. Yet, without clear supervisory directives to explicitly incorporate the four key ingredients of PJ into POP interventions, or write-ups of POP projects explaining exactly what elements of PJ were used, we—as consumers of these reports—are left in the dark. The real potential of POP for fostering legitimacy is thus unknown at this point.

Summary Comments

We started this chapter with the idea of trying to decipher whether there were subtle differences in the relative impact of different types of police interventions on citizen perceptions of police and/or the impact on crime. Our results show three things: First, the overwhelming majority of studies that evaluate police interventions that include PJ elements and measure legitimacy-enhancing outcomes show that there are very few downsides to PJ policing. Second, it is really too close to call as to which of the different types of vehicles generates the best legitimacy-enhancing outcomes: They all do and the available evidence is too patchy to try to rank order police interventions by which is best and which is worst in terms of achieving the best legitimacy-enhancing outcome. Third, the variable impact of legitimacy-enhancing police interventions on crime outcomes creates more questions than it answers. The relative impacts of the instrumental (i.e., performance and effectiveness) and the process models of policing are, indeed, a complicated story (Jackson et al. 2012; Murphy et al. 2008; Sunshine and Tyler 2003; Tankebe 2009a).

Chapter 4
PJ Dialog for Frontline Police: Introducing QCET

Introduction

Doing procedural justice (PJ) is largely about dialog. Without negating the fact that two-thirds of communication is nonverbal (see Hogan and Stubbs 2003; Pease and Pease 1994), the spoken word during police encounters with citizens is what doing PJ is all about. What police say, how they say it, and the manner in which people interpret the language of the encounter lies at the heart of the PJ dialog. Regardless of the vehicle in which PJ policing is delivered (see Chap. 2), the dialog component of frontline police–citizen encounters is important for promoting citizen satisfaction, trust, compliance, and cooperation with the police, and for enhancing perceptions of PJ and police legitimacy (see Chap. 3 and Mazerolle et al. 2013a). The take-home message here is this: PJ dialog is good, but too much dialog might annoy citizens and end in a negative, backfire effect.

Bottoms and Tankebe (2012) focus our attention to the dialogic importance of PJ policing, drawing on the scholarly work of Weber (1978), Beetham (1991), Coicaud (2002), and Walzer (1994). For Bottoms and Tankebe (2012, p. 141), authorities "… must derive their authority from, and act within, the shared beliefs and values of a given society." Legitimate power holders communicate shared beliefs through the dialog they incorporate into their interactions with citizens. Consequently, ongoing claims to legitimacy from the power holders (i.e., the frontline police) and iterative responses from citizens mean that "legitimacy needs to be perceived as always dialogic and relational in character" (Bottoms and Tankebe 2012, p. 129).

The goal of this chapter is to show how we translated the theory of PJ dialog into practical words as part of the Queensland Community Engagement Trial (QCET). We begin by providing background to the development of QCET. We then discuss the concept of dialog and the importance of structured dialog. We then recap each of the ingredients of PJ and describe how we deliberately sought to foster legitimacy in QCET through careful crafting of structured dialog. We provide some of the basic findings from QCET and conclude this chapter with ideas for how police and scholars might nurture the dialogic nature of legitimacy in different contexts with different interactions. We find that PJ dialog is useful, but too much dialog might have a backfire effect.

L. Mazerolle et al., *Procedural Justice and Legitimacy in Policing*,
SpringerBriefs in Criminology, DOI 10.1007/978-3-319-04543-6_4,

The Starting Point of QCET

Following the systematic search of legitimacy policing in 2008–2009, Bennett and her colleagues (2009) showed that the literature lacked a randomized field experiment that operationalized (i.e., put the principles of PJ into practice) and tested the basic causal relationship between the four key elements of PJ and police legitimacy. Despite decades of research using observational and survey data that showed the relationship between PJ and legitimacy, the basic cause–effect relationship of the combined power of the four PJ ingredients had never been tested under experimental field trial conditions. Subsequent to the completion of the systematic search, Lorraine Mazerolle secured significant funding from the Australian Research Council Centre of Excellence in Policing and Security (CEPS) to conduct a major field trial of PJ. The Queensland Police Service (QPS), as a CEPS partner, expressed interest in exploring how police agencies could use PJ to better engage with the community. The field trial was designed to test the cause–effect relationship between the four key PJ ingredients, operationalized as a script, and citizen perceptions of police legitimacy (Mazerolle et al. 2012, 2013a).

From the outset, Assistant Commissioner (AC) Peter Martin of the QPS viewed high-volume random breath testing (RBT) as an ideal setting for administering the PJ script (Martin 2012a). In Australia, roadside RBTs—which involve a quick, 20 s encounter where the driver is asked by the police to blow into a handheld blood alcohol calibrating machine—are a commonplace tool for curbing drink driving. In Queensland alone, some three million RBTs are undertaken each year, representing a ratio of one test per one licensed driver. RBTs represent a high-volume police–citizen encounter in Australia aimed at reducing the number of accidents and fatalities caused by drivers under the influence of alcohol and/or drugs. RBTs are similar to what police in the USA call a "roadblock." AC Martin understood that RBTs allowed police to interact with a cross section of society and a large portion of the community who are otherwise unlikely to come into contact with police. He also believed that Queensland drivers could be better utilized in helping the QPS reach its crime prevention goals.

During routine RBTs (that became the QCET control, business-as-usual condition), police deliver a succinct and direct mandated message:

> My name is [rank and name] from [specific traffic branch]. You have been stopped for a random breath test. I now require you to provide a specimen of breath for a breath test. This is a breath testing device. To comply with my requirement, I direct you to place your mouth over the mouthpiece of the device and blow directly and continuously through that mouthpiece until told to stop by me.

The PJ approach (experimental condition) was developed as an add-on to this standard script in such a way that it could stimulate structured PJ dialog between police and drivers during routine RBTs.

What is Dialog?

In its simplest form, dialog is a conversation (oral or written) between two or more people. Unlike a debate, in which conversation is closed and competitive, dialog is open, neutral, and suspends opinion, resulting in shared understanding (Glover 2007). Discussions that are founded on dialog can lead to a "tough on issues but gentle with one another" approach where participants are encouraged to appreciate multiple perspectives in addition to their own (Glover 2007, p. 61). Harvey (2005) argues that dialog is particularly necessary in situations where conflict abounds to enable participants "…to explore individual and collective values, reach shared understanding and identify action in integrity with that understanding" (Harvey 2005, p. 1). According to Isaacs (1999), dialog can be used to evoke trust and dissolve fragmentation.

"Dialogic leadership" extends the basic notion of dialog. In dialogic leadership, the leader ensures that the dialog includes four elements: providing people with "genuine voice," listening "deeply," respecting others' views as valid, and broadening awareness and perspective (Isaacs 1999, p. 2). These ingredients align succinctly with the core ingredients of PJ and bring to light how the structure of dialog is critically important for facilitating legitimacy. The key here is that it is the job of the dialog "leader"—in this case, the frontline police officer—to structure the dialog and ensure that the exchange is delivered in such a way that it carefully pays attention to the four components of PJ: neutrality, dignity and respect, voice, and trustworthy motives.

Structured Dialog

Structured dialog involves using more efficient and effective dialog to gain cooperation and resolve problems when multiple perspectives are involved. Unlike semi- or unstructured dialog, structured dialog ensures that the participants (police and citizens) follow a formalized process of dialogic exchange, focused on a specific problem with clear objectives and outcomes. In QCET, for example, the outcome of the dialog was both the required breath specimen to assess whether the driver had been drinking and the opportunity for the driver to offer police insights into what they felt should be crime prevention priorities for the local area. With QCET dialog, as with all dialogic exchange, the component parts need to be well defined, transparent, and involve active participation (with adequate representation, leadership, and capacity) and shared understanding (Civil Society Helpdesk—CiSocH 2011).

In a general sense, structured dialog is particularly useful in complex situations where all stakeholders' views must be heard equally (see, for example, European Commission 2012). An evaluation of the European Commission's aid delivery suggests that structured dialog is a key turning point in participatory development and cooperation. Thus, depending on the complexity of the problem to be reviewed, or the range of participants involved, the structured dialog can be designed to utilize an assortment of tools (e.g., technology and graphics) to enable understanding and respect, as well as to achieve consensus and action (Christakis and Bausch 2006).

Unlike many practitioners, frontline police rarely get the opportunity to use tools to help with structured dialog. An exception, perhaps, is online, real-time access to crime mapping where clusters and hot spots of crime events can help structure the dialog during routine encounters. With ready access to technology such as smart phones and tablets, these crime maps are increasingly available for police to use in the context of their routine, structured encounters with citizens. In the remainder of this chapter, we explore the development of the QCET police dialog that aimed to increase perceptions of legitimacy during routine police–citizen encounters.

Development of QCET Script

Martin and Mazerolle worked together to determine how routine RBTs could be adapted to incorporate the key attributes of PJ. The goal was to develop a consistent PJ script that police could deliver at the point of the RBT traffic stop with a view to engaging drivers in a procedurally just encounter. The basic idea was to capture the four elements of PJ as well as meet the requirements of the police (mandated RBT message) in a realistic script that police could deliver comfortably and stimulate PJ dialog. When reflecting on his contribution to the PJ script development, AC Martin (2012b) stated: "My thoughts were that it would be important for police to really make a connection with the motorist…. In the context of a brief intervention—such as an RBT—this connection had to be established very quickly and be meaningful."

The PJ script development for the RBT encounter was an iterative process. AC Martin (2012b) worked with the QCET research team over a number of weeks to ensure the script was not too "clinical and perfunctory," was meaningful to police, and equated to real engagement. Iterations of the dialog involved broad consultation with research staff, senior police, and operational police officers. Each reviewer considered how best to operationalize each of the elements of PJ into a structured script that could be reasonably delivered within the context of the RBT encounter. In the following section, we describe how the four ingredients of PJ (recall these are neutrality, trustworthy motives, dignity and respect, and voice) were carefully crafted into a police dialog for the experimental condition.

Neutrality

The QCET team (including both police and researchers) determined that the best way to demonstrate neutrality was to emphasize the randomness of the RBT. RBTs are, by nature, intended to be random (Homel 1988): The RBT roadblock is configured to pull over clusters of motorists. Cars are pulled over in groups of between four and eight cars at a time. At each RBT roadblock, a cluster of cars is directed to the roadblock area where a "line" of six, seven, or eight officers each attends to a car and asks drivers to blow into a calibrated testing device in order to give a breath specimen.

In QCET, the police emphasized the random nature of the RBT roadblock. Police told drivers that they were pulled over at random and had not been specifically targeted or profiled for the test. Randomness was conveyed in the QCET script as a proxy for neutrality as follows:

> We are pulling cars over today at random. That means that you were not specifically singled out for this test. We are randomly testing drivers for alcohol use so that we can reduce the number of alcohol-related traffic crashes on our Queensland roads.

Trustworthy Motives

Demonstrating trustworthy motives was easy to operationalize within QCET. In Australia, newspapers routinely print the cumulative count of traffic fatalities and all Australian police agencies articulate traffic fatality targets, with significant resources dedicated to reducing the road toll each year (Queensland Police Service 2012). The traffic police in Queensland are generally passionately invested in reducing the number of accidents and fatalities on the road. Within QCET, police communicated how much they cared about the road toll and how these incidents affected them. Police aimed to personalize their encounters with drivers by asking them to drive safely and responsibly—the implication was that the police were invested in keeping the specific driver safe on the roads. Trustworthy motives were thus communicated in the QCET script like so:

> In Queensland alone there were 354 deaths in 2009. One of the hardest parts of our job is to tell a person that their loved one has died or has been seriously injured in a traffic crash.
>
> Can you please help us to reduce these accidents by continually driving carefully and responsibly?

Voice

In contrast to our efforts to operationalize neutrality and trustworthy motives, incorporating "voice" into the PJ script presented a challenge. Voice involves citizen participation in decision making. In QCET, we struggled to think how we might give motorists voice when they are legally required to submit to a breath test. After considerable deliberation, the QCET team included an opportunity in the script for citizens to ask questions about the department's crime prevention priorities, talk about what they saw as important priorities for police, and discuss the types of things they did to prevent crime. To promote voice in the structured dialog, police were scripted to communicate their current approach to crime control priorities, elicit concerns from the driver about what they saw as priority local crime problems, and seek new ideas for crime prevention from the motorists. Police officers thus invited motorists to engage in a dialog about what the police were doing and what each party could do better in regard to crime prevention.

AC Martin (2012a) explained that the aim of the "voice" part of the script was to empower the motorist in the exchange by giving them information and encouraging them to join with police in discussing crime prevention priorities. Extracting voice during the dialog was attempted in two ways: First, police were scripted in the QCET dialog to offer a crime prevention "tip" to the motorist. The tip was not intended to be one way. Rather, the crime prevention tip was meant as an icebreaker to get the motorist to talk about crime prevention. AC (Martin 2012a) provided one example that was used often during the QCET dialog:

> When a citizen had a portable navigation aid attached to the vehicle then the officer could say something like, "I see you have a portable navigation device. Just a reminder to you that when you stop at your destination you might want to put that out of sight. We don't want someone breaking into your vehicle to steal it. We would be grateful if you would work with us to prevent crime. Protecting property is one of our key priorities and we don't want you to be a victim of crime."

Second, police were scripted in the QCET dialog to discuss the crime prevention priorities of the police department. To help the conversation along, a one-page crime prevention flyer was given to the driver (Mazerolle et al. 2013a, 2012). The flyers contained a monthly count of offenses occurring in the local police district, crime prevention events coming up, and a list of the different things police were doing to reduce crime. Officers were encouraged to focus their crime prevention dialog around the crime prevention flyer as a way to elicit "voice" from the driver.

Dignity and Respect

The final ingredient of PJ is dignity and respect. Operationalizing dignity and respect needed to be both explicit and implicit. Implicitly, the police working in the experimental QCET condition were trained and monitored to use polite words and engage body language (such as crouching down to be at eye level with the driver) during encounters. The QCET script also incorporated a specific message of dignity and respect. At the end of the RBT encounter, officers thanked motorists for their time and found something positive to say to each driver. For example, some officers thanked motorists for ensuring children wore safety belts. AC Martin (2012b) stated:

> Police should leave motorists feeling not only empowered after the exchange with the officer but in a positive frame of mind.... I held the view that if the exchange was structured to focus on a positive dimension of the encounter then it followed that the motorist would have similarly positive views about the officer and about the institution of policing.

AC Martin (2012b) added that "...everyone wins when the conversation is positive and police recognize good practice from a member of the public." He imagined that QCET might encourage officers to feel good about the transaction and positive about the message and the experiment. In the long run, AC Martin hoped that this RBT dialog might eventually become self-sustaining.

The Prompt Cards and Bringing Oneself into the Dialog

The QCET research team from the University of Queensland (UQ; see Mazerolle et al. 2011b) developed a double-sided prompt card for officers to guide their structured dialog with motorists. On one side of the card was a scripted example of a complete interaction involving the full PJ dialog. On the flip side, the dialog was abbreviated, with simple prompts that officers could tailor for individual interactions. In providing and encouraging officers to use the prompts—as opposed to the full-scripted dialog—we hoped that the officers would maintain a sense of autonomy and be more likely to engage with the process. In effect, we hoped that by giving "voice" to the officers, we would increase their buy-in to the experimental dialog.

When reflecting on the QCET script, AC Martin (2012a) observed:

> The scripting was very, very important. But I think that if you give people the scripting, and if you tell them what you want to achieve, and if you give them the theoretical framework as to why they are doing what they are doing, then you also give them the confidence to use the script as the basis for a conversation.

He added:

> ...we wanted them [our officers] to be dealt with in a fair and transparent manner...we really wanted people to understand the process. So we built those procedurally just planks into the script, but wanted them to adapt the script and put it into their own words (Martin 2012a).

QCET Roll Out

After conducting a pilot test of the proposed experimental condition, the QCET team (see Mazerolle et al. 2011b) developed a case flow system to randomly allocate 60 roadside RBT operations to control (business-as-usual) and experimental (PJ) conditions. The trial ran from December 2009 to June 2010 in the southern suburbs of the City of Brisbane (Queensland, Australia). With over 20,000 breath test stops and distribution of the same number of surveys given to motorists, the trial involved over 30 traffic police officers and a sworn Inspector from the QPS. The Inspector worked closely with the police RBT units and the UQ research team to ensure that the trial met both police operational standards and the conditions of a randomized field trial.

A comprehensive survey incorporating PJ and legitimacy constructs was developed drawing on seminal work by Murphy and Mearns (2008) and Tyler (1997, 2003, 2004, 2008) and colleagues (Tyler and Fagan 2008; Tyler and Huo 2002; Tyler and Wakslak 2004). Drivers were asked about the purpose of RBTs, driver attitudes toward drinking and driving, perceptions of the RBT stop and the quality of their interaction with the police during their encounter, their general perceptions of police in Queensland (e.g., "the police treat people with dignity and respect"), neighbors' perceptions of the police (e.g., "people in my neighbourhood think that police are fair"), levels of community engagement (e.g., "I feel strong ties to others living in my local neighbourhood"), and demographic questions. No directly identifiable information was requested and completion of the survey was voluntary. The survey also gathered citizen demographics, how they felt generally about the police, information about previous engagements with police (including past offenses), and some questions about their perceptions of their own community and what they saw to be crime and disorder problems in their community. A copy of the full survey can be found at Mazerolle et al. (2011b).

Key Findings from QCET

Across the 60 operations, a total of 20,985 surveys were distributed to drivers, with approximately 13 % returned to the research team (a total of 2,747 surveys across the experimental and control conditions). In the experimental condition, there were 1,645 returned surveys and 1,102 in the control condition, indicating a slightly higher response rate in the control condition (13.73 % control vs. 12.30 % experimental). Overall, just over half of respondents were female, with equivalent numbers of males and females in the control and experimental groups. The ages of respondents ranged from 17 to 90 years, and the average age was 47.25 years, with no significant differences between experimental and control groups. Australian ancestry (including Aboriginal and Torres Strait Islander ancestry) was the most common ancestral group (49.17 % of respondents), followed by European (39.50 %), Asian (5.00 %), and countries geographically close to Australia (i.e., New Zealand, Melanesia, Micronesia, and Polynesia; 3.74 % of respondents). The remaining respondents identifying as African, Middle Eastern, or from the Americas comprised 2.60 % of respondents. Further details of the survey sample can be found in Mazerolle et al. (2011a).

Analysis of the returned surveys showed that the PJ encounter had far-reaching and positive effects on citizen perceptions of police. Drivers who received the experimental RBT encounter—the PJ encounter—were 24 % more likely than the control group to report that their views on drinking and driving had changed. Citizens receiving the experimental condition also had more positive perceptions of police. We found significant differences between the experimental and control groups on all key outcome measures: Experimental respondents reported small but higher levels of compliance and satisfaction with police during the encounter than did their control group counterparts (see Fig. 4.1). These and other findings from QCET are published in Mazerolle et al. (2012, 2013a) and Murphy et al. (in press).

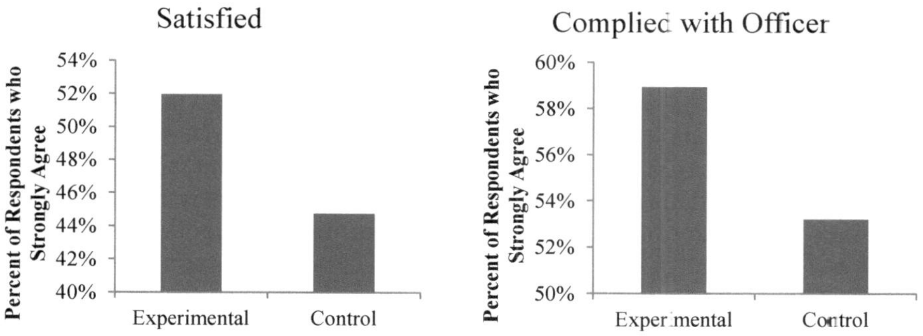

Fig. 4.1 Percentages of respondents who were satisfied and complied during RBT encounters

Future Directions

QCET involved a specific type of police–citizen encounter at RBT sites. The RBTs are a forced encounter—motorists are required by law to pull over, listen to police, and, upon direction, blow into a tube connected to a calibrated breath-testing device. In this sense, the balance between authority and audience was disrupted. Despite the specific nature of the RBT encounter, we learned a lot about the application of PJ to police–citizen dialog. As the breath test occurred following delivery of the PJ script, we hoped that motorists would view the mandatory, legally required breath tests as legitimate. Our experimental results support this conclusion (see Mazerolle et al. 2012, 2013a). Compared to motorists in the control condition (i.e., those who received only the short and perfunctory QPS mandated statement prior to the breath test), drivers in the experimental condition (i.e., those who engaged in the PJ dialog) viewed the officers they encountered as more legitimate (see Mazerolle et al. 2013a). Murphy et al. (in press) also found that the PJ dialog promoted greater trust in police (we know from Chap. 1 that trust is one important element of police legitimacy). QCET thus provided a short and targeted dialog to test, experimentally, whether the use of PJ ingredients in a short dialog (cause) could impact on specific and global perceptions of legitimacy (effect).

Another aspect to QCET and the PJ dialog is the extent to which the longer experimental dialog generated the legitimacy-enhancing effect or whether it was simply the longer time the police spent engaging with citizens. In Mazerolle et al. (under review), we find that there is a "Goldilocks" effect to the positive responses provided by motorists in the experimental condition related to the length of time of a QCET encounter. Encounters lasting about 2 min seemed to produce the most positive response from drivers. By contrast, when police spent too long (i.e., too far over 2 min), engaged in PJ dialog with drivers, drivers reported less favorable attitudes toward the police. The take-home message here is this: PJ dialog is good, but too much dialog might annoy citizens and end in a negative, backfire effect.

Everyone is busy, and chitchat from police that is purposeful, engaging, and respectful is a good thing. But police need not go overboard.

We recognize, however, that there are many more—and arguably more meaningful—police–citizen encounters where PJ dialog could be used than in the RBT encounters. For example, we envision that an effective structured dialog could be used to improve victims' satisfaction with police encounters and their willingness to report repeat victimization, to reduce calls for service in domestic violence situations, to reduce harm and conflict in watch houses, and during police responses to break and enters, and in a myriad of other police–citizen encounters. We hope that future QCET replications (see Chap. 7) might advance our understanding as to how dialog (structured or unstructured) is fundamental to the theory and practice of PJ. Such future research could untangle whether some of the key ingredients of PJ are less important than others, or whether all four must be used together to be effective. It may be the case, for example, that interactions involving less or no voice, but more dignity and respect, could generate greater citizen perceptions of legitimacy. Our QCET study delivered the procedural script as four essential "ingredients" (Goodman-Delahunty 2010).

Chapter 5
Trials and Tribulations of Doing PJ: The Black Box of QCET

Introduction

Procedural justice (PJ) is a key antecedent of legitimacy. PJ dialog emphasizes four key features—voice, neutrality, dignity and respect, and trustworthiness—during police–citizen encounters (Tyler 2008; Tyler and Huo 2002). As outlined in Chap. 1, research finds that PJ enhances police legitimacy and public cooperation with police, among other outcomes (Murphy et al. 2008; Sunshine and Tyler 2003; Tyler and Fagan 2008).

The PJ-based model of policing is, in the extant academic literature, contrasted with the performance-based model. The performance-based model of police legitimacy focuses on more instrumental outcomes such as crime reduction, criminal detection, and the provision of police services, with emphasis on fighting crime and maintaining community safety. Police roles and functions use the performance-based model to shape operational objectives of police agencies, using this model to elicit community cooperation through the threat of detection and apprehension (Bayley 1994; Murray 2007; Scott 1998). While the performance-based model has merit, it can be costly to maintain and can undermine the willingness of groups to cooperate with police (Cherney and Murphy 2011; Sunshine and Tyler 2003).

PJ research indicates that police need to change how they go about fulfilling their various roles and functions, in particular by focusing less on the instrumental dimension of policing and by acting in ways that are procedurally fair. The challenge in doing so cannot be underestimated because established operating procedures can present barriers to reforming existing police policies and practices to ways that emphasize PJ. That is, moving from a performance-based model to a PJ-based one can pose some challenges.

In this chapter, we aim to shed light on the potential difficulties that can arise when integrating PJ into police policy and practice. We do so by reflecting on the challenges encountered during the implementation of the Queensland Community Engagement Trial (QCET). In Chap. 4, we demonstrated that operationalizing the key ingredients of PJ can be challenging. In this chapter, we draw on survey data of the population of all police members who participated in QCET, and in-depth interview data with senior police and academics responsible for managing the trial

L. Mazerolle et al., *Procedural Justice and Legitimacy in Policing*, SpringerBriefs in Criminology, DOI 10.1007/978-3-319-04543-6_5, and getting it up and running. Our discussion thus reflects upon the experience and observations of people involved in the implementation of QCET. We suggest that the challenges encountered in implementing QCET are not only relevant to similar experimental trials but also pertinent to the integration of PJ into police practice. In this chapter, we open up the "black box" of QCET to explain the contingencies and barriers encountered during implementation of the trial. Such detail has often been lacking in experimental research (see Tilley and Pawson 1997). Moreover, given that there have been few attempts to field-test PJ, an account of QCET's implementation has value in providing practical lessons for police and academics interested in evidence-based policing.

Implementation Challenges of Doing PJ

Prior to implementation, QCET police and researchers worked through a number of logistical issues. The most pressing issue was to select the area of police operations suited to a PJ trial. As discussed in Chap. 4, AC Martin recommended targeting random breath testing (RBT). At first, the RBT context appeared to lack the emotionally charged elements that characterize particular police–citizen encounters (i.e., it could only provide a partial test of the capacity of PJ to temper public reactions to the police). However, RBTs did offer a range of unique advantages. To begin with, RBT operations provided the necessary case flow to conduct a suitably powered experimental trial. RBTs also provided the opportunity to test the applicability of PJ to a high-frequency police–citizen encounter involving a cross section of the community, thus providing scope to test the generalizability of the approach.

Several different types of RBT operations were considered for the trial: The QCET team considered doing the trial around individual officers' RBT ad hoc encounters, or around large, full-scale encounters on freeways using what is colloquially known as the "booze bus." The team finally decided on "middle-range" RBT operations as the most appropriate. These middle-range operations occur in a specific location at a designated time (most often on a weekend) and offer the necessary volume of RBT operations to allow allocation to experimental and control conditions (the experimental condition involved delivering PJ dialog to citizens—see Chap. 4 for a more detailed outline of the experimental and control conditions utilized in QCET). To ensure adequate sociodemographic variations (e.g., ethnic minorities) among treatment and control sites, police and researchers selected heavily suburbanized police districts for the trial. Once these initial decisions about the target and location of the trial were settled, a number of additional contingencies were addressed to ensure that the principles of PJ could be tested in a live experiment. Each of these issues and obstacles are outlined below.

Securing Police Support for the Trial

Adopting a new innovation or practice presents challenges for any organization. Implementing changes can be difficult, given the established ways of operating (Cherney and Head 2011; Rogers 1995). This is no different for police agencies. From the outset, QCET researchers needed to convince senior police that a PJ trial had merit. Gaining the support of organizational leadership proved essential for the success of the trial. This task was made easier given the established relationship between the senior academic leading the QCET research (Mazerolle) and the Assistant Commissioner (AC Martin) heading the Ethical Standards Command, which also had oversight of all research within the police agency. The working relationship between Mazerolle and Martin was important for the implementation of the trial as there was an established foundation of trust and familiarity upon which aims, priorities, and needs could be discussed and negotiated to achieve mutually beneficial outcomes for police and researchers.

Organizational leadership was essential to generating the necessary momentum for undertaking a PJ trial. This required senior police taking carriage to secure support for the trial across the Queensland Police Service (QPS). In other words, it required an insider to champion the initiative and act as a change agent. This was not just about persuading police that a PJ trial had merit; it was also about convincing police of the benefits of applying it to a particular area of policing (i.e., RBT) that had been conducted in the same way for decades. AC Martin, who took on this leadership role, described this process in the following way:

> I was of the view that police officers would respond really poorly to a suggestion that they do random breath testing in a different way. So I knew that I would have very significant obstacles to overcome at the operational level; but also too, structurally…. So that required some fairly careful negotiation with my colleagues and the senior executive to actually encourage them to see the utility and the merit of what we were trying to do, so that we could actually get them on board to facilitate the trial…some of the arguments I was proffering, was around the notion that we have undertaken business in this way for a long period of time. It's returning a road safety dividend, presumably, but we might be able to achieve significant other benefits—multiple benefits—for the same initiative if we just take an innovative and different approach…my major plank in my argument was about doing things different; asking ourselves what could be the potential for a different way of doing business and were there other benefits that we could accrue as a result of doing this.

Convincing police about the merit of a PJ trial did not end with senior executives in the QPS. Winning over rank-and-file officers was also important, given the potential demands the PJ condition placed on officers to change the standard dialog delivered during an RBT operation. Ensuring officer compliance with the PJ condition (i.e., the PJ script) was important both to the integrity of the trial and in ensuring that there was a substantive change in the way police engaged with motorists. Doing so required that a senior officer with operational experience was present at all times during the 30 experimental RBT operations:

> The real important issue was to make sure a senior person at inspector level was embedded into every one of the teams [i.e., RBT operations]—experimental and control side—when they went out and deployed; injected themselves into the process so that they could give a briefing in terms of what was proposed and what the expectations of officers was and moreover, if they saw an individual departing from the scripting, that what they could do [was] inject themselves into the process and, ultimately, stop, cause a cessation of that sort of behavior and put them back on track.... If we hadn't have applied that particular strategy I don't know it would have been possible to have succeeded. (Senior police commissioned officer involved in QCET)

Achieving Ownership and Winning Support Among the Rank and File

For PJ to become universally delivered in mainstream policing, it needs to be widely embraced by operational police. Officers must be open both to changing their methods of community engagement and to shouldering the added task of acting with procedural fairness alongside sometimes competing priorities (e.g., responding to a required number of calls for service or processing a certain volume of cases). Research on community policing and problem-oriented policing illustrates the difficulties involved in gaining support for such innovations among rank-and-file police (Scott 2000; Skogan and Hartnett 1997). The same applies to PJ policing (Scott 2000; Skogan and Hartnett 1997).

For QCET, once the logistics of allocating RBT operations to control and experimental conditions had been formulated, a number of engagement ("winning over") strategies were initiated. The goal was to encourage support for the trial inside the chosen police districts. In order to encourage their support, members of the academic research team and a senior police officer seconded to the QCET project (a police Inspector) met with district commanders and traffic police to explain the aims of the trial. Before each operation, the Inspector assigned to QCET, in an effort to "rally the troops," briefed police assigned to the experimental sites and thanked them for their participation. At first, police in these districts were intrigued by the notion of PJ and the purpose of the trial, and in most instances were willing to participate because police members with authority and seniority were supporting the trial. Over time it became clear, however, that operational police were ambivalent about the trial, expressing some resistance to what they regarded as an imposition on how they conducted RBTs. This resistance arose for a number of reasons, which are discussed in the following sections.

Integrating PJ into Existing Practice

When designing the PJ dialog it was important to consider the length of each PJ-infused conversation. By law in Queensland, police are required to provide a very specific instruction to motorists when requesting a breathalyzer test. Police undertaking RBT operations have, over many years, become very efficient in delivering this verbal instruction. The average time police spend on an individual RBT encounter during business-as-usual (control condition) is 20 s. Moreover, the pressure for RBT operations to be efficient is compounded by performance indicators specifying the required number of motorists to be processed through an RBT operation. An RBT operation typically lasted for 5 h of an 8-h shift, where some 400 motorists are tested over the 5-h period. Adding the key ingredients of PJ to each standard RBT encounter significantly extended the length of each RBT encounter, which translated into significant reductions in the overall number of motorists processed during a 5-hour RBT operation. Police executing the experimental condition did not regard the longer encounter *and* the fewer number of motorists tested for drink driving as desirable. Police were also skeptical of the value of engaging motorists in an extended dialog that departed from their more clinical, detached approach to engaging with the public. The Inspector seconded to the QCET described this problem in the following way:

> …These guys [in reference to the traffic police]—they do it like clockwork. I mean for the purposes of research I'm not going to paint a false picture. There is a requirement under law, which is based simply on case law, where there are particular requirements, what police officers are required to deliver to the driver is very much set out. It's very, very specifically articulated what has to be said…. A good example will be you'll often come to instances where they'll say this is an RBT, just blow into the tube for me. That's not sufficient. It's not sufficient technically under law, because there have been so many case examples over the years, where case law has now been developed where people have been able to argue, appropriately and correctly, that they weren't given a proper direction. So if they're not given a proper direction they can refuse…. We now strictly demand that they give exactly the right requirement. It takes a bit of practice to get the speech off…. Where the tension arises is when I've asked them to now introduce the intervention…. Now I came along and I ask them now, particularly now on the experimental group, to introduce a whole new pattern…. Most of them had difficulty memorizing it [in reference to the PJ dialog] because they do this from—machine like, they get out there and they're very quick. I'm asking them to interfere with their processes that they've used before. There was a bit of tension in the sense that some thought it was, I suppose, straight out a little cheesy. They thought, well we're not going to say all this nonsense. Others thought what right have we got to hold people up that long, what's this going to achieve.

Officer resistance was exacerbated by a perception that engaging the public through a PJ dialog was in conflict with one of the key priorities of an RBT operation—catching drink drivers. Traffic officers in the experimental condition struggled with the idea that engaging the public could have the broader dividend of improving police legitimacy. To the traffic officers, their core function was to detect and deter drink driving. The general view was that these aims could only be achieved if a high volume of motorists were processed through an RBT operation in the allocated amount of time. This was held up as an important value by police operating the RBTs and central to their sense of purpose and perceived effectiveness. It resulted in officers judging the PJ dialog as an "unnecessary distraction." Also, some officers saw community engagement as "someone else's responsibility," which only added to the perception that conversing with the public through a PJ dialog was "not real police work." As the Inspector working on QCET put it: "I had a few of them who said to me—quite literally they said this is a load of wank. I said well to you it might be, but not to the public."

Below are some comments from the survey that police officers made about the experimental condition that illustrate officer resistance to the QCET experimental condition.

- To detect drink drivers, we need to get the volume of traffic through RBT sites. The exercise of talking (conveying impact of drink driving) should be relayed through the department of crime prevention.
- It's a good op, but it's too slow and we miss out on numbers.
- RBTs should be about random breath testing, not other policing issues. Drink drivers are being missed as a result of this current trial.
- Process was very time consuming and made it less likely to identify drink drivers.
- This is the most inappropriate use of resources I have ever struck in 20 years with the QPS. RBT is an effective tool against drink-driving and this ridiculous waste of time serves no purpose except to self-serve somebody's agenda. Let police officers police. RBT is too important to mess with.
- This should be about deterring drink driving.
- It is irrelevant and embarrassing lecturing innocent motorists.

Resistance, Legal Challenges, and the Impact on Officer Behavior

The perceived incompatibility between the objectives of PJ and its adoption in the RBT context led to resistance to the trial among some police officers. While the trial plans received consistent support of senior police, this resistance to the trial before it even commenced gained momentum when the police union was drawn into the process. Police from one of the districts that had participated in the pilot test of the experimental condition and were due to participate in the full trial approached their union representative and argued that the experimental condition was unlawfully detaining motorists for an excessive period of time. One line of argument presented against the trial starting was that it presented legal risks. In relation to the legal challenge mounted against QCET, a senior police executive involved in the trial stated:

> Well, before the trial got under way, I was aware of a groundswell of angst that had started to manifest itself, particularly around the notion of what we're doing here in this experimental side, is we're taking longer to process people, therefore we're not being—we're not able to stop as many vehicles as otherwise we would stop. Therefore, the presumption is we're letting drink drivers go. These drink drivers are going to go down the road and, potentially, they could kill themselves or other people and we're going to be legally liable.

This reaction was not unexpected among the police planning QCET, and the team moved quickly to quell any overt resistance to the trial. This included seeking independent legal advice about the trial condition, meeting with union representatives, and making a commitment to police officers that any liability lay with senior police. The legal challenge was overruled by the QPS and the trial started on schedule.

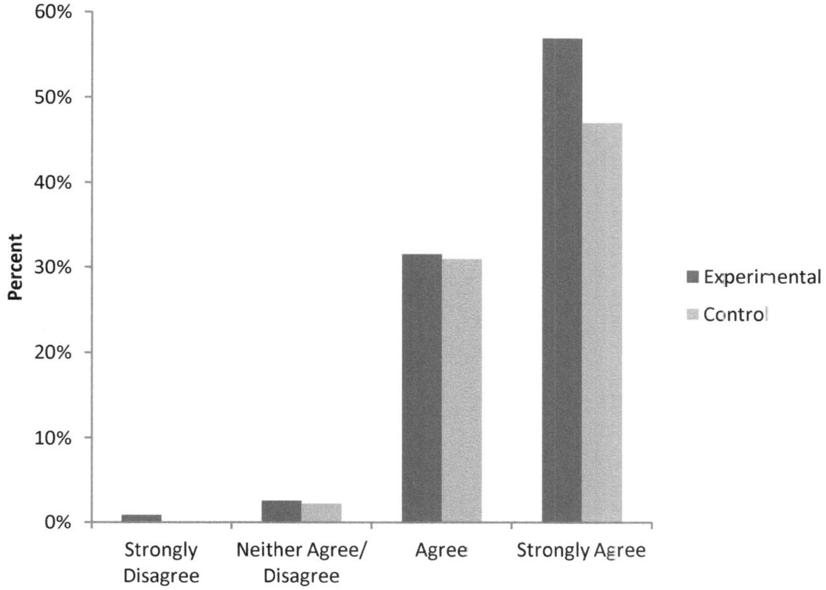

Fig. 5.1 Officer survey (N=175): Thinking about today's RBT, do you think you were approachable and friendly?

Despite problems associated with achieving "buy in" among rank-and-file officers, data show the trial condition did have an impact on public perceptions of police legitimacy (Mazerolle et al. 2013a). Mazerolle et al. (2013a) found that those in the experimental condition of the QCET (where the PJ script was delivered) had more positive perceptions of police legitimacy. Also, data from the officer survey distributed to police in control and experimental sites indicate that some police did see merit in the PJ approach. For instance, one officer stated: "This RBT session [the experimental condition] was quite good. Could relax and speak with drivers instead of just doing RBT numbers." The Inspector seconded to the QCET also believed officers may have been enjoying the experimental condition:

> I think they [i.e., police] were a bit afraid to tell their mates they were enjoying it, but you could see how some of them were just all over it [in reference to the PJ dialog], really enjoying the day. Some even quietly said to me it's nice to be able to just talk to them for a change [i.e., motorists].

A comparison between officers in the experimental and control conditions does show that officers judged the PJ condition as having an impact on how they engaged the public compared to normal RBT operations. Figure 5.1 shows that officers in the experimental condition were more likely to agree or strongly agree that they were approachable and friendly in the operation. Figure 5.2 shows that officers in the experimental condition were more likely to think of themselves as being fair in the operation.

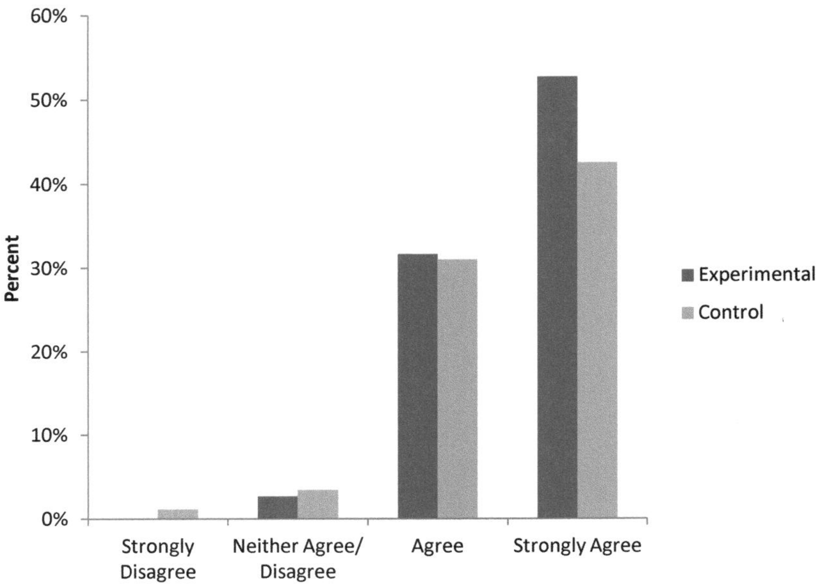

Fig. 5.2 Officer survey ($N = 167$): Thinking about today's RBT, do you think you were fair?

Maintaining the Integrity of the PJ Encounter

Enabling police to integrate PJ practices in tandem with the right to use discretion presents a challenge, and imposing a certain level of prescription on how police employ PJ raises the question of monitoring. Any attempt to do so may be resented by police officers who view monitoring as undermining their discretion and independence. Compounding this problem is the fact that we do not actually know the weight or relative importance of the four different components of PJ. Beyond being an important research question, it becomes a major issue if police adapt, or even jettison, certain ingredients of PJ depending on the circumstances they face at any given time. As such, imposing PJ policing may be unrealistic, but allowing for flexibility in its adoption could threaten the integrity of the PJ approach. Finding a solution to this challenge is not easy, particularly in view of the uncertainty around which features of PJ matter the most and in what circumstances.

This issue of maintaining the integrity of the PJ dialog was considered during QCET. An inspector attended each and every one of the 60 RBT operations in the trial (30 experimental and 30 controls) and researchers were also assigned to monitor each operation, even though they were mindful to avoid the impression of constant monitoring and scrutiny. However, some police officers resented attempts to control and monitor their behavior during the RBT encounter: "I have been doing this job for a long time and never before have I had to have someone behind me while I do my job. I find this belittling and demeaning" (quote from QCET police officer survey).

Overseeing the police–citizen encounters was not only about maintaining the integrity of the experimental condition, but it was also about ensuring that the principles of PJ were reflected in how police undertook RBT. There was a need to accommodate preferences and allow for individual adaptations of the PJ script to ensure it could be easily integrated into existing police practice. This balance between sticking to the script and allowing for interpretation was described by the Inspector seconded to the QCET in the following way:

> It was critical that the message had to get across—it had to look like or sound like it was the officer personally taking an interest in the individuals, not I'll just read this to you. Now we had a couple of officers who had great difficulty memorizing the content. I can understand that people have trouble with things like that. So unfortunately for the entire duration of the six months I recall one particular officer just simply putting the card in his hand [in reference to the PJ script] and read it straight to them. I didn't intervene with that, I didn't say don't do that. I asked him was he having difficulty with it and he said not really, I just find it easier to read it. I said well if you feel you're getting the message across to the people you're talking to you do whatever suits you…. Other officers were very, very good, they never looked at it once [i.e., the PJ script]. They'd start the shift, have a quick glance at it, and put it away. I'd stand quietly behind them as I was walking along, not to linger too long, but to listen to them. (Police Inspector seconded to QCET)

A member of the academic research team talked about the PJ dialog in the same way:

> The script was important, in that it captured all the ingredients—because if you missed out on one of those, in our mind, you hadn't delivered that experimental condition, or that particular intervention. So the script was very, very important. However, we were…certainly open to some stylistic changes…. I just remember one of the officers saying, listen, this is just too dense [in reference to the procedural justice script], and I remember having a conversation saying, well, why don't I just stick it into some dot points…we played around with a couple of different options. (Member of the QCET academic research team)

Public and Media Reactions

Research indicates that particular groups or individuals may be less interested in whether or not police treat people with PJ (e.g., Murphy and Cherney 2012; Tankebe 2009b). PJ also does have the potential to increase the length of police–citizen encounters (as observed in QCET), which members of the public are not accustomed to. Individuals or groups may subsequently find these encounters inconvenient. Moreover, they may become suspicious about why the police are interested in their opinion, despite the more positive experience PJ attempts to generate between police and the public. People may be more interested in the police "catching crooks" than in dignified and respectful treatment. Such attitudes can be reinforced by the nature of media reporting about police and reactions to alternative policing approaches.

News of QCET was made public in a Brisbane newspaper under the headline: *Police ask drivers at RBTs whether they are being friendly enough* (Dickinson 2010). This was in reference to questions in the motorist survey distributed to drivers when processed through the experimental and control sites. The article stated that neither the Queensland Police Media unit nor the Police Minister at the time would take responsibility for the survey. The article itself made no mention of the fact that the survey was connected to an attempt to test a new police practice that might have broader dividends for the police.

Public indifference about the intent of the trial was also reflected in written comments by police in the officer survey that members of the public regarded the PJ encounter as an inconvenience and were not interested in engaging with police. One of their concerns was that the longer experimental and PJ-scripted version of the RBT would become a standard operating procedure at the conclusion of the trial. This concern generated a number of negative comments about what police thought the public felt about the experimental operations, which are listed below:

- 50 % in a rush just wanted the test
- Generally listened but most just wanted it done quickly
- Most could not care less
- Most people were angry and stated this was a waste of time

This negative feedback does not mean that the QCET police were wasting time and resources when adopting PJ. Indeed, as noted elsewhere in this chapter, some police in the PJ condition welcomed the opportunity to engage more actively with the public. Furthermore, data demonstrate that compared to the control, the experimental condition significantly produced higher perceptions of police legitimacy (Mazerolle et al. 2013a) and trust in police (Murphy et al. in press). Despite these findings, the reality is that any commitment police make to strategies based on PJ will be influenced by media and public reactions, given that police agencies are sensitive to how the media and public perceive police policies and practices.

Summary Comments

It could be argued by some that the lessons learned and outcomes from QCET are not transferable to other policing contexts. The trial was introduced into a very controlled and contained police–citizen encounter that lacked the unpredictability and volatility of other forms of police–citizen contacts. For other types of police–citizen encounters that are more emotionally charged, the approach and outcomes could be very different. Viewed in another way, the very fact that PJ matters in routine (and mundane) encounters (as found in QCET) may highlight its importance for provocative situations. Only future research will tell. Whether or not the findings can be generalized, lessons learned from QCET's implementation will be important to consider for future adoption of PJ-policing strategies. QCET shows that fair policing requires an understanding of how police organizations operate and the culture within different police units. QCET faced challenges at all levels within the QPS, where efforts to enhance the normative dimension of policing in one particular operational area conflicted with existing practices and priorities. In the PJ literature, there is a lack of consideration of how you can take the theoretical concept of PJ and integrate it into police policy and practice. QCET provides insight into this challenge.

Chapter 6
Barriers to Implementing PJ

Introduction

In Chap. 5, we examined the challenges of encouraging police to innovate and adopt practices based on the principles of procedural justice (PJ). Future efforts to transform police policy and practice in line with a PJ-based model of policing can learn from the Queensland Community Engagement Trial (QCET) experience. In Chap. 5, we brought to light various contingencies that make the integration of PJ dialog into police practice less than straightforward. We continue this theme in this chapter by examining barriers to institutionalizing PJ as part of mainstream police organizational policy and practice and highlight the complexities of the PJ approach for some people in the community.

If the efficacy of PJ rests on the adoption of its four key elements—trustworthiness, respect and dignity, neutrality, and voice (see also Chap. 1)—then this approach should be adopted with fidelity by police, rather than cherry-picked in a way that avoids any major change to existing practice. Unfortunately, organizational factors operating within policing agencies can inhibit the reliable uptake of innovative strategies that draw on the PJ-based policing model. Dominant methods for delivering police services, measuring police performance, and managing rank-and-file officers may be entrenched practices that are difficult to shift or reform (Graziano et al. 2013). In addition, external factors pertaining to public and political demands on police can undermine innovation in policing. In this way, police may be locked into the instrumental, performance-based model of crime control, where the focus is on detecting and apprehending lawbreakers, rather than considering how crime reduction can be achieved through alternative and potentially less adversarial means.

While there is clearly merit in considering what inhibits the uptake of a PJ-based policing model, we also caution against the uncritical adoption of PJ. There may be contexts and situations where it does not work, or even where it is counterproductive. The level of enthusiasm expressed among scholars for the PJ approach means that potential limitations have been rarely considered (see, for an exception, MacCoun 2005). In addition, PJ is not necessarily applicable or even realistic in all contexts, given the nature of police–citizen encounters and situations in which police operate and make decisions. For some communities and groups, PJ may not

L. Mazerolle et al., *Procedural Justice and Legitimacy in Policing*,
SpringerBriefs in Criminology, DOI 10.1007/978-3-319-04543-6_6,

be at the forefront of their expectations about police behavior (Murphy and Cherney 2011; Sargeant et al. in press). Individuals could regard opportunities to have a "voice" in police–citizen encounters as simply a strategy to co-opt compliance with police directives, rather than as a sincere effort to allow citizen input in decision making (Cherney and Murphy 2011, 2013; Murphy and Cherney 2011; see also Cropanzano and Ambrose 2001 as it relates to organizational decision making).

This chapter divides the impediments to implementing PJ into four areas: external and political, organizational, individual, and community-level barriers. For the purpose of this chapter, we discuss each issue separately, but recognize that they are not mutually exclusive: The political domain will influence organizational practices in policing, which will impact the behavior and decisions of individual officers.

External and Political Barriers

In the past, police budgets were largely quarantined from government cutbacks. The government's attempts to reduce expenditure on policing were met with criticism by the media, opposition parties, and police unions citing deleterious impacts on police effectiveness. In the present day, skyrocketing government budget deficits mean the police, like many publically funded services, are increasingly subject to austerity measures and are required to reevaluate the provision of services (Police Executive Research Forum 2013). In response, police have amalgamated police units and in some cases reduced the number of senior executive and administrative positions in an effort to maintain or even bolster frontline policing. Police justify this shift in focus as getting "back to basics," emphasizing the traditional crime-fighting role of the police. In consequence, approaches like PJ can be criticized and dismissed as "namby-pamby" (Hough 2013, p. 195) or "touchy-feely" policing. From this perspective, approaches based on dialog, engagement, and consultation are not seen as part of police core business and can be pushed aside. Community policing is an example of how an otherwise successful innovation can become, over time, a marginalized approach within police agencies. Community policing is, however, one area where the principles of PJ have been emphasized or could be strengthened (see Chap. 2, see also Cosgrove and Ramshaw 2013).

Alternatively, Hough (2013, p. 195) argues that austerity measures in policing may present more, rather than less, avenues for PJ to be integrated into police practice. PJ policing may in fact offer opportunities to achieve "more with less" (Hough 2013, p. 182). This is derived from the fact that how police decide to treat and interact with the public is completely under police control, and PJ approaches to engagement can help to secure greater levels of public cooperation. Hough (2013, p. 181) suggests that "… procedural justice may be able to gain more traction in times of austerity, given that changing policing style does not necessarily incur significant costs." While we agree with Hough's conclusions, the demands placed on police to facilitate a PJ approach should not be underestimated. As indicated in Chap. 4, the length of police–citizen encounters is often increased under a PJ model. Despite the tipping point of PJ encounters—where extending the PJ encounters for too long can end up frustrating citizens (see Mazerolle et al. under review)—we are hard-pressed to imagine a PJ encounter taking less rather than more time. Moreover, when police are placed under increasing pressure to achieve value for money in service delivery, anything that adds to the time they spend on particular duties and distracts them from detecting and apprehending criminals may be set aside—no matter how beneficial an approach might be to improving public support for the police.

The dominance of the performance-based model of policing (i.e., eliciting compliance through the threat of detection and apprehension of lawbreakers) is also a barrier to the uptake of PJ policing because it accords with political and media discourse surrounding crime control and the need to "get tough" on crime. Showing sympathy and respect for criminals, suspects, or nonmainstream groups does not accord with the dominant exclusionary "us and them" or "thin blue line" mentality underpinning law and order (Garland 2001; Scheingold 1984). PJ encompasses a very different style of policing, requiring police to rethink how they achieve compliance and change their role from law-enforcer to someone who seeks input into police decision making through dialogic processes. The PJ model requires that police deliver respectful treatment to all, even criminals. Politicians, fearful of being seen as "soft on crime," are less likely to value and support approaches based on trust, dialog, and reciprocity. Hence, the broader political landscape surrounding public debates on crime control and policing can deter police from investing in alternative strategies that potentially recast their roles and functions away from hard-nosed approaches to those that are more benevolent in orientation.

Organizational Barriers

The social psychological literature on organizational justice shows that the way people are treated in the workplace has a major bearing on whether they accept and comply with organizational processes and policies (Colquitt et al. 2001). Research finds that the fairer managers treat their staff, the more likely staff are to commit to the goals of the organization they work for and to accept senior decision making (Bradford et al. 2013; Colquitt 2008; Colquitt et al. 2001). This has implications for how police agencies adopt PJ. For instance, as we discussed in Chap. 1, it is going to be difficult to convince police officers about the merits of PJ if the approach is not adopted within the institution of policing by senior police managers and leaders. That is, senior staff should use PJ when engaging with their subordinates. The impact of PJ is reciprocal and self-reinforcing, in that the more you observe and experience it, the more likely you are to apply it in your own interactions (Colquitt et al. 2001).

Research to date focuses primarily on the external benefits of PJ: how it helps to enhance police legitimacy and cooperation among members of the public. While there is a growing body of research that examines organizational contexts more generally (see Chap. 1 for more detail), few studies examine PJ from an organizational perspective in relation to its benefits within police agencies. A study conducted by Myhill and Bradford (2013) in the UK involved a survey of 1,697 police members (including community support officers and police volunteers) about their judgments of organizational justice and attitudes toward organizational policies, goals, and serving the community. Measures of organizational justice were based on questions relating to perceived fairness in provision of training, performance appraisal, career development, and how receptive police members felt senior officers were to their views and opinions. Myhill and Bradford (2013) found that perceptions of organizational justice influenced positive attitudes toward the organization and its aims, as well as support for community policing and helping members of the public. Other research also shows that when police hold positive perceptions about organizational justice within their workplace, they are more likely to act ethically (Bradford et al. 2013; Wolfe and Piquero 2011).

Scholarly interest in PJ shows, we suggest, that PJ relates not only to how police treat the public but also to how police are treated internally by senior decision makers. In this regard, we also note the impact of organizational culture. Scholars suggest that the policing occupational organizational culture is split into two, along hierarchical lines, resulting in a management cop culture and a street cop culture (Paoline 2004; Reuss-Ianni 1993). These groups have very different views about each other's roles and functions and the goals of policing (Paoline 2004; Reuss-Ianni 1993). This split can create an "us and them" mentality between senior police and rank-and-file officers, and a sense that neither appreciates nor understands each other's perspectives (Reuss-Ianni 1993; Toch 2008). Such social distance between the senior members responsible for developing policy and the officers who are required to implement it makes the transmission and uptake of any new practice difficult (Skogan 2008; Toch 2008). Also, given the hierarchical nature of police agencies, a key priority of senior police managers is to maintain tight oversight and control over operational policing, which can generate a top-down approach to police reform (Toch 2008). This can lead to rank-and-file officers feeling their opinions and thoughts do not count, and that their leaders are not interested in what they think about operational decision making. A lack of voice (recall voice is a key element of PJ), and tight oversight, implies officers are not trusted or valued, which undermines judgments about organizational justice (Colquitt et al. 2001; Saunders and Thornhill 2003; Toch 2008). In consequence, police can feel PJ is not a key priority within their workplace, which can negatively impact on how they engage with the public (see also Bradford et al. 2013).

Any reform or call for police to change their roles and functions is typically coupled with demands that police training needs to be improved (Bradford and Pynes 1999). The same applies to PJ (Tyler and Huo 2002), with efforts in the UK underway to integrate PJ into police training (Quinton et al. 2012; Wheller et al. 2013). While such developments are welcome, the already overloaded police training curriculum means finding space for nontechnical skills related to PJ, such as problem solving, judgment and engagement, is difficult (Buerger et al. 1999). This has been observed in relation to the introduction of problem-oriented and community policing training (Birzer 1999, 2003; Bradford and Pynes 1999). The problem is that police training primarily focuses on the mechanical and technical aspects of policing (e.g., firearms training, defensive tactics, driving, and the mechanics of arrest; Birzer 1999, 2003; Bradford and Pynes 1999; Buerger et al. 1999). Practices focused on improving community engagement and public cooperation are often left to "learn on the job" when they could be incorporated as part of the formal training curriculum (Buerger et al. 1999). Arguably, this type of training should be incorporated when officers are inducted. After all, any change to police practice needs to occur from the bottom-up, which requires that officers be schooled in PJ before they engage with the public.

Individual Barriers

The context and dynamics of police–citizen encounters make the uptake and application of PJ challenging. The nature of these interactions needs to be fully understood when considering the use of PJ. It is important to recognize, therefore, that during police–citizen encounters, the inherent conditions of human interaction (i.e., reciprocity and exchange) are absent (Alpert and Dunham 2004; Manning 1977). During these encounters, police officers generally attempt to maintain a level of control over the interaction in order to achieve a particular outcome. The citizen desires to preserve a sense of identity in a context where deference to an officer's legitimate authority is assumed by police (Alpert and Dunham 2004; Sykes and Clark 1975).

When police demonstrate PJ in their interactions with the public, it can help generate deference to police authority, particularly through exchanges that display respect for a person or group. However, interactions between police and citizens can digress into an authority maintenance ritual, where officers assert their power to demand compliance from citizens (Alpert and Dunham 2004; Sherman 1993; Sykes and Clark 1975). This can see a ratcheting-up of more coercive forms of compliance to ensure obedience is forthcoming and respect for police is maintained (Alpert and Dunham 2004; Sherman 1993; Sykes and Clark 1975). The problem is that strategies like PJ can be regarded as a sign of weakness by police officers. PJ requires police to display a benevolent, caring stance through open displays of respect, even for individuals who challenge police authority (Alpert and Dunham 2004; Manning 1977; Sykes and Clark 1975). Police can view this as undermining their ability to maintain their authority edge in interactions with the public (Alpert and Dunham 2004; Manning 1977; Sykes and Clark 1975). The existence of such negative attitudes among police about noncoercive forms of compliance is supported by research on police use of force options (Alpert and Dunham 2004). Hence, PJ may not fit well into the types of authority maintenance rituals that police adopt during police–citizen encounters.

PJ has the capacity to transform police–citizen interactions and avoid defensive, volatile, and combative encounters (Sherman 1993). However, in Chap. 1 we demonstrated how PJ can even be useful when police are interacting with victims of crime and people with mental illnesses (see Mastrofski et al. 1996; McCluskey 2003; Mccluskey et al. 1999; Sherman 1993). Yet, some circumstances may not warrant, or be predisposed to, PJ. Take, for example, the case of police dealing with people under the influence of drugs or alcohol. Under these circumstances, cognitive impairment may mean a person is not receptive to respectful treatment, or opportunities to voice their opinions or to explain why they are involved, for instance, in a violent incident or disorderly conduct on the streets. Here, safety (of the public and police), rather than PJ, will be the central consideration for the officer. The same argument could be made in the context of arresting a violent offender. Under some circumstances, police may have no alternative but to physically restrain or otherwise apply a range of lethal and nonlethal use-of-force options. It is an overstatement to say that PJ can improve cooperation, without understanding or appreciating the contexts under which police must elicit cooperation, and whether it is possible through noncoercive means.

PJ can generate higher levels of police legitimacy and cooperation with police; however, there is not always an immediate and identifiable outcome resulting from that cooperation. Outcomes of PJ can be more diffuse—the public may simply express greater confidence in the police. This can be problematic for individual officers. For example, if police are evaluated on crime control outcomes, rather than on the way they treat citizens, PJ will be a less attractive option. Moreover, when police are used to operating in a particular way to meet particular goals (e.g., as was experienced in QCET in relation to traffic police and random breath testing (RBT)), reforming practices that are entrenched over time can create a high workload for officers, who can become fatigued from the need to engage with the public via PJ methods.

Community Barriers

Prior research finds that PJ is generally important for minority groups in terms of predicting perceptions of legitimacy and cooperation with police (see, for example, Bradford and Jackson 2010; Sunshine and Tyler 2003; Tyler et al. 2010). As explained in Chap. 1, prior research in the UK and the USA suggests that the PJ-based model of legitimacy is similar for minority and majority groups. However, emerging research in other countries indicates that the impact of PJ on police legitimacy and cooperation may not always be uniform across social groups (Cherney and Murphy 2013; Jackson et al. 2013; Michael et al. 2012; Murphy and Cherney 2012; Sargeant et al. in press; Van Craen 2012a). For instance, research in Australia shows that for some individuals (particularly those from minority groups) PJ is not the most important factor in influencing their support for, or willingness to cooperate with, police (Murphy and Cherney 2011, 2012). Murphy and Cherney (2011, p. 248) found that "procedural justice might be less effective in shaping cooperation among minority group members than for majority group members." Similarly, they found that PJ might actually have a counterproductive effect on cooperation with police when minority group members question the legitimacy of particular laws they are being asked to obey (Murphy and Cherney 2012, p. 194). It also appears that for some cultural groups police performance matters more than PJ when making judgments about police legitimacy and deciding to cooperate with police (Sargeant et al. in press). One explanation of this phenomenon is that minority communities often experience strained relations with police and feel they are poorly served by them (Bowling et al. 2003; Brown and Benedict 2002; Brunson and Miller 2006; Meredyth et al. 2010; Röder and Mühlau 2012; Van Craen 2012b; Warren 2010; Weitzer and Tuch 2006). When they do not expect fair treatment, they may become more concerned about whether police are effective at controlling crime in their neighborhoods (i.e., outcomes relating to police performance; Murphy and Cherney 2011; Tankebe 2009b). Research in Ghana has suggested that where citizens presume the police are corrupt and incompetent due to a historical legacy of human rights violations, extrajudicial killing, and institutional corruption, personal safety is an issue and hence crime control is crucial (Tankebe 2008, 2009b, 2013). This may overshadow concerns about PJ in some contexts.

Judgments about police legitimacy and the willingness to cooperate with police are also influenced by one's sense of identity and connection to society. For majority groups who identify strongly with the dominant culture (e.g., identifying with American society, as opposed to identifying with a minority group), assessments of institutional authorities like the police are often more strongly influenced by relational factors about how the police engage, interact, and consult with the public (Huo 2003; Tyler 2006b; Tyler et al. 2000). This is because they have a strong sense of connection with the broader society and believe institutions like the police serve their interests (Tyler 2006b). On the other hand, people who identify less with the dominant culture and its institutions place a greater social distance between themselves and authorities, meaning they are far more disengaged from the police and are more suspicious and distrusting of them (Braithwaite 2010; Cherney and Murphy 2011; but see Murphy 2013). Hence, PJ may have a lesser impact on police legitimacy and cooperation (or may even have a counterproductive affect) in these contexts (Braithwaite 2010; Cherney and Murphy 2011).

What does this mean for the adoption of PJ in practice? Research indicates that, overall, PJ matters for most people; however, in some contexts the story may be different. First, in some community contexts, PJ may not be effective because some minority communities, who are already distrusting and suspicious of police, may not react favorably to PJ. As argued by Cherney and Murphy (2011), it can be hard for police to overcome poor community perceptions simply through PJ policing, with groups seeing PJ as an insincere and cynical attempt by police to gain cooperation (see also Brandl et al. 1994; Hawdon 2008). This is compounded by direct and indirect experiences with police that shape public attitudes (Barrett et al. 2013; Hawdon 2008). Negative contact with police or a story about police mistreatment against one's racial or ethnic group can outweigh positive exposure because it reinforces preexisting negative attitudes about police (Barrett et al. 2013; Skogan 2008). Hence, improving community cooperation and engagement with ethnic minority communities, youth, or other disenfranchised groups may require more than simply the application of PJ to overcome negative attitudes toward police or an unwillingness to cooperate. For this reason, it is also crucial that police do not use a facade of PJ to generate cooperation from citizens. Unless police are genuine, individuals might mistakenly believe they have a voice in police decision making, when in actual fact they have no chance of influencing the outcome. If police manipulate PJ in this way, it has the potential to further entrench negative attitudes, as citizens become aware that their input has no influence, reinforcing preexisting views that police are disengaged and "don't care" (MacCoun 2005; Murphy and Cherney 2011).

Police must also contend with the legitimacy of the law (Cherney and Murphy 2013; Dixon 1997; Murphy et al. 2009). Viewing the police as legitimate does not necessarily translate to viewing the laws police enforce as justifiable or fair. This is problematic for the police. It will be difficult for police to generate cooperation if the laws they are enforcing are not seen as reasonable or justified. Research shows that "law legitimacy" has a bearing on police legitimacy and the willingness of citizens to cooperate with police (Cherney and Murphy 2013; Jackson et al. 2012; Murphy and Cherney 2012; Murphy et al. 2009). It is inevitable that people will see particular laws as unreasonable infringements on personal freedom (e.g., laws relating to speeding and seatbelts, laws that restrict gun ownership). However, there are circumstances where community backlash against certain laws is undesirable and can undermine police effectiveness. Take, for example, the issue of counterterrorism policing. In this context, Muslim communities find themselves under increased police attention and surveillance due to Islamic-inspired terrorism. This has led police to form community-based partnerships with Muslim communities to prevent radicalization (Lambert 2011; Pickering et al. 2008; Silk et al. 2013). Unfortunately, while Muslim communities might see the police as legitimate, they may continue to view counterterrorism laws and policies as biased because they believe police unfairly target Muslims and label them as "suspect communities" (Pickering et al. 2008; Sun et al. 2011). This makes the formation and sustainability of meaningful community-based partnerships against radicalization difficult (Lambert 2011; Silk et al. 2013; Spalek 2012).

Counterterrorism laws and policing have also generated community backlash and disengagement among Muslims, leading to the questioning of police authority and withdrawal of cooperation (Lambert 2011; Pickering et al. 2008; Silk et al. 2013; Sun et al. 2011). Given the unprecedented legal powers of police to preempt terrorist acts, the broader legal context in which the police operate can undermine community cooperation (which is essential for mitigating the risks of terrorism and radicalization; Pickering et al. 2008; Silk et al. 2013). Research does indicate that the perceived legitimacy of the law among Arabic-speaking groups in Australia influences cooperation in counterterrorism policing (Cherney and Murphy 2013). The lesson here is that improving police–citizen cooperation is not simply about how the police act toward members of the public (i.e., in a PJ manner), but it is also about whether the legal instruments the police use are seen as legitimate (Cherney and Murphy 2013).

Summary Comments

The arguments put forth in this chapter do not discount the benefits of PJ in relation to improving police legitimacy and helping police to win the trust and confidence of the communities they serve. Doing so is central to policing by consent (Goldsmith 2005). However, translating PJ into practice can involve confronting barriers. We believe PJ scholarship has not given enough consideration to this issue in the field of policing. Police face many competing pressures, which are sometimes incompatible: Giving consideration to PJ during police–citizen interactions is but one of many issues police must consider. The political, organizational, individual, and community contexts in which police work and encounter different members of the public means that the application of PJ must compete with a range of other demands and processes. Hence, the high expectations, among scholars and advocates, which surround the applicability and adoption of PJ need to be tempered. We must recognize the contingencies that constrain the implementation of a PJ-based policing model. However, there are particular factors and circumstances that do help facilitate the uptake of PJ by police organizations: We consider these in Chap. 7.

Chapter 7
Scaling Up and Expanding Out: Future Directions for PJ in Policing

Introduction

In this monograph, we have outlined the merits of police legitimacy and its key antecedent: procedural justice (PJ). It is clear that there are aspects of police policy and practice where this approach can be integrated, such as community policing and problem-oriented policing (see Chap. 2). The experience of the Queensland Community Engagement Trial (QCET; Chaps. 4 and 5) shows the challenges associated with changing a particular area of policing in line with PJ, but that doing so will have positive implications for citizens' perceptions of police. If PJ policing is to progress beyond one-off experiments, the barriers outlined in Chap. 6 should be considered. With this in mind, this chapter examines the minimal conditions needed to support the integration of PJ into mainstream policing and proposes some ideas for moving forward with PJ in policing. We begin with a discussion of organizational features, then examine the important role of training, and conclude with the topic of QCET replication and directions for the future.

Organizational Support and Compatibility

Emerging literature across the fields of knowledge and change management, institutional and organizational learning, the diffusion of innovations, social psychology, and research utilization examines what is termed the "knowledge-to-action" (KTA) process (Cherney and Head 2011). This field is primarily concerned with understanding how to take research and evidence (such as that based on PJ) and integrating it into policy and practice. Studies in the field of implementation science have also begun to shed light on how to "scale up" programs tested through experimental designs across large populations and within multiple contexts (Flaspohler et al. 2008; Welsh et al. 2010). This literature provides important lessons and insights for evidence-based policing and how a PJ-based policing model can be supported and adopted across police agencies.

L. Mazerolle et al., *Procedural Justice and Legitimacy in Policing*, SpringerBriefs in Criminology, DOI 10.1007/978-3-319-04543-6_7,

Drawing on this literature, we identify a number of supporting conditions for the "scaling up" of PJ. First, police agencies must invest in activities to improve knowledge about and understanding of PJ and its key principles. These communication strategies should be directed toward new recruits during training, as well as toward more seasoned police officers. The focus should be specific to operational areas. Police should be provided with information about PJ specific to their roles and functions, and how these should be fulfilled. As indicated in Chap. 5, PJ training may struggle to gain traction within certain operational areas, if it is not seen as compatible with the aims of the existing practice. Police need to be competent in the execution of PJ dialog, and scripts and training will be important tools to ensure the uptake of PJ policing (see Chap. 4 and below). However, there should always be flexibility in how PJ is integrated into police practice. As indicated in Chap. 6, there are certain contexts and groups where it may not be appropriate or may be less effective. Discretion is an important part of policing that should be retained.

PJ policing is concerned with ensuring that police engage with the public in a way that enhances the quality and outcomes of police–citizen interactions. Implementing PJ policing will therefore have implications for internal organizational processes. This pertains to both the way PJ is incorporated into strategies such as community policing and the way in which senior and rank-and-file police interact with one another. As argued in Chap. 6, there is a reciprocal relationship between adopting PJ, both within and outside the organizational context: If police are accustomed to observing PJ in their interactions with others within the organization, this will flow into how they interact with the public (outside of the organization). For the successful uptake of PJ in police–citizen interactions, the organizational structure of the police service needs to be compatible with the principles of PJ (i.e., voice, dignity and respect, neutrality, and trustworthy motives; Cherney and Head 2011).

Police need to treat all individuals as valued members of society. While this might seem obvious, the treatment of individuals can have broader implications. Research tells us that any negative experience, or act of force against an individual, can erode public trust and confidence in the police and undermine police legitimacy (but see Skogan 2006). To ensure PJ is applied across the board, policy that embeds and reinforces PJ as part of an ethos of customer service should be implemented (e.g., through customer service charters or strategies). Solidifying the importance of PJ in police–citizen interactions into policy will not guarantee that all police officers will adopt such principles; however, it does set an overall standard that should underpin operational policing.

The application of standards that are commonplace in policing should also be applied to the formation of police–community partnerships. Unless police are open to input from the public and are willing to involve citizens in the decision-making process, partnership policing is largely an empty gesture. While there are undoubtedly situations where this may not be possible, police should recognize that public consultation (i.e., voice) without any demonstrable input and outcome could be viewed as more unfair than no consultation at all (Cherney and Murphy 2011; Murphy and Cherney 2011).

Finally, police leaders should champion PJ and the PJ-based policing model across their respective agencies. The literature on the KTA process demonstrates that new innovations must be supported and endorsed by senior leaders who are willing to argue for its adoption and support its integration into operational policy (Cherney and Head 2011). The QCET experience illustrates this point, in that it is unlikely the trial would have occurred if not for the endorsement of senior members of the Queensland Police Service. If these senior police officers had been unwilling to confront and address resistance to the implementation of QCET, the trial would not have been successful (see Chap. 5). Such organizational champions must also act as mediators between academic researchers in the PJ field and the translation of research evidence into policy and practice. For example, these organizational champions can help to translate PJ research into workable and practical principles that make sense to police personnel. However, these champions are unlikely to succeed without achieving organizational legitimacy in the first instance (Cherney and Head 2011; Greenhalgh et al. 2004). Moreover, they will need to possess experience that reflects an appreciation of the contingencies police face when putting PJ into practice.

Training

Police–citizen interactions can shape perceptions of police. As such, training police in the use of PJ in interactions can help to improve public perceptions of police. Many police agencies do already (informally or formally) designate a part of their internal training to teaching skills in citizen engagement. However, more attention could be given to training police in PJ more specifically. There are a number of examples that show how police can improve the quality of police–citizen encounters and engage with the public in a more meaningful way. These range from general (e.g., leadership training) to more specific instructions (e.g., training targeted at encounters with specific disadvantaged or vulnerable groups). This section describes some of these approaches.

As indicated in Chap. 6, the policing of particular groups (e.g., ethnic minorities, or those with mental and/or cognitive deficits) sometimes presents a challenge for policing. Training that provides police with an understanding of the particular needs of specific (and often unfamiliar) disadvantaged or vulnerable groups, in specific contexts, can help police to respond to future encounters with these groups more confidently and with less force. Citizens with an intellectual disability may not, for example, have the same knowledge of the criminal law, in terms of what constitutes an offense committed by or against them, nor fully understand their legal rights. In addition, an intellectual impairment may result in a person poorly articulating his or her needs or responding to police in a manner (e.g., aggressively) that is out of context with the situation, which can lead police to escalate their use of force. Brennan and Brennan (1994) report on the "Cleartalk Project" aimed at developing training for police to recognize and effectively communicate with people with an intellectual disability. The training scheme, which involves police actively reflecting on and discussing communication concepts among colleagues and trainers (e.g., questioning strategies and communication tools) and building in systems to assess communication effectiveness (e.g., asking individuals to repeat back in their own words, why certain questions have been asked, and what will happen next), incorporates ingredients of PJ.

Mentoring less-experienced police officers is an integral part of a senior officer's role, and provides essential on-the-job training for junior officers. As already indicated, senior police can promote PJ policing in how they treat and interact with colleagues. This can have an impact on how junior police interact externally with members of the public. Berringer (2004) found, for example, that transformational leadership styles—where leaders strive to positively influence beliefs, values, and morals of officers—had more of an impact on officer behavior than laissez-faire or transactional styles that focus primarily on seeking compliance with expectations about particular group norms.

An important consideration in officer training is recognizing where there may be points of divergence between the aims of training and organizational values or targets. This was raised in Chap. 5: What might be important to police effectiveness, such as enhancing police legitimacy, may not be what evaluations of police performance (e.g., arrests or convictions) are based on.

Another example of efforts to train officers in PJ is the Chicago Quality Interaction Program (QIP; see Rosenbaum and Lawrence 2013; Schuck and Rosenbaum 2011). The randomized design involved recruits, matched on demographic characteristics (gender, race, age, and prior military background), being assigned to receive either the QIP training or standard academy training (see Rosenbaum and Lawrence 2013; Schuck and Rosenbaum 2011). One component of QIP training was to encourage the growth of a new police culture that endorsed key PJ principles and promoted effective interactions premised on the notion of "treating others how you want to be treated." The QIP curriculum placed an emphasis on providing opportunities for recruits to engage with instructors and receive tailored feedback on their performance of key tasks during police–citizen encounters. The training aimed to enable officers to resolve problems in the quickest amount of time and with minimal effort and use of force, while utilizing PJ. Training modules included the use of written scripts on how to display the principles of PJ during police–citizen encounters, interpersonal communication and decision-making skills, cultural awareness, and stress management using case studies, scenarios, role-playing, and simulations. Evaluation of QIP showed that it did improve new recruits' interpersonal attitudes and skills, with the training having a positive impact on recruits' decision making in conflict scenarios with youth, and with QIP-trained recruits showing more respectful and supportive behavior (see Rosenbaum and Lawrence 2013; see Schuck and Rosenbaum 2011).

As mentioned in Chap. 6, there have been efforts within UK police agencies to implement training on PJ. One example is the training in the Greater Manchester Police (GMP) that was accompanied by a randomized controlled trial on police officer training undertaken by the UK College of Policing (Wheller et al. 2013). Designed as a strategy to improve victim satisfaction and public perceptions of the

GMP, the trial aimed to test whether training on PJ could improve the way police interact with the public. Officers were recruited to participate in training aimed at improving effective communication when dealing with members of the public, particularly victims of crime. The training was delivered either as 2 days of classroom learning, 2 days of classroom training with an additional 1 day of active scenario-based training, or as 1 day of classroom training and the additional day of scenario-based training. Officers who received training were compared to a control group of officers who did not receive any such training.

The training package explained the value of "customer service" when dealing with members of the public. While officers were instructed in the use of standardized scripts, they were also encouraged to develop more personalized dialog, with training aimed at providing officers with a range of communication techniques that could be used flexibly in different encounters. Classroom-based learning focused on communication techniques to enhance skills in expressing empathy, rapport, and positive acknowledgments (e.g., acknowledging victims' feelings); signposting (explaining available options to reduce unrealistic expectations); using names (both officer and individual); using phrases that focus on expressing what the officer can do for the victim, rather than saying "no"; and encouraging officers to seek feedback from victims on whether they have been helpful. Scenario-based learning focused on enabling officers to practice these techniques, reflect on the scenario (which was videotaped), and receive one-on-one feedback about their performance.

Evaluation of the training program involved comparing officers who took part in these training sessions with a control group of officers who did not undergo the additional training. All officers (both trained and untrained) participated in a videotaped role-playing scenario 3 months after the training occurred to test its impact on officers' behavior in a police–citizen interaction. Officers who received training had more positive attitudes toward delivering quality service, the importance of building empathy and rapport, and fair decision making, compared to officers who did not participate in the PJ-based training. Follow-ups of victims who had contact with treatment group officers reported they were treated fairly. Due to insufficient numbers of officers, the effects of the different deliveries of the training package were not analyzed separately, though there is tentative evidence that the impact of the training on outcomes might have been reduced if the scenario-based learning, where officers were able to practice their learnt skills in a safe environment, was not included. Overall, findings from the trial showed that the PJ training intervention, regardless of delivery style, had a consistent and positive impact on officer attitudes and behavior and victim perceptions (Wheller et al. 2013).

Replications of QCET

Integrating PJ into police policy and practice requires a willingness on the part of police to try out various aspects of the approach and test its use and applicability to different operational areas. Undertaking experiments similar to QCET is one way in which police can test innovations aimed at improving how they engage with the public and their legitimacy. However, as outlined in Chap. 5, such trials are characterized by certain challenges. While experimental trials are seen as a central part of evidence-based policing (Sherman 1998), whether or not there are organizational capabilities and support within police agencies to undertake such trials cannot be overlooked.

Replications of trials like QCET play an important role in providing evidence of the need to incorporate PJ into operational policing. Each successful replication provides additional information that such approaches work and can work in varying contexts. Replications based on experimental methods help to test whether a police innovation can work in similar situations or with other participants. One of the first replications of the QCET experiment occurred during 2012–2013 in Richland County, South Carolina, in the USA, undertaken by Prof. Geoffrey Alpert and Assistant Prof. Jeff Rojek at the University of South Carolina in partnership with the Richland County Sheriff's Department. In South Carolina, traffic stops are less regular and less routine than in jurisdictions such as Queensland, though they are still a relatively common police–citizen encounter. The replication involved training officers in PJ through the use of a scripted dialog when they were stationed at sobriety checkpoints (similar to random breath testing (RBT) stations in Australia). Drivers were issued a paper survey, with an online survey also used to help boost response rates. Overall, the study involved 45 checkpoints, encountering 2,225 drivers. Similar replications are occurring in Turkey and Scotland (in the context of roadside vehicle safety checks), and in New Zealand, police are also examining how to integrate PJ into road policing.

One would hope police are persuaded by research evidence that PJ has an impact on enhancing public cooperation and improves police legitimacy. The challenge is how to operationalize such an approach, given that its impact may not be the same across all groups and contexts (see Chap. 6). Trials like QCET and its experimental replications help us to further understand the application of PJ.

Concluding Comments

In this chapter, we have canvassed the conditions and processes that can help take PJ from an empirically supported concept to a mainstay of police work. This requires organizational support, training, and willingness on the part of police to test and replicate PJ effects in different operational settings. We do not discount the challenges that confront police in adopting PJ, but given the potential benefits that can result in improving both police effectiveness and police legitimacy, it is not something that should be relegated to the "too hard basket." It is hoped that ideas discussed in this, and previous chapters, shed light on how PJ can be scaled up and made part of mainstream policing.

References

Alpert, G. P., & Dunham, R. G. (2004). *Understanding Police Use of Force: Officers, Suspects, and Reciprocity* (Vol. Book, Whole). Cambridge: Cambridge University Press.

Barrett, G. A., Fletcher, S. M., & Patel, T. G. (2013). Black minority ethnic communities and levels of satisfaction with policing: Findings from a study in the north of England. *Criminology and Criminal Justice*. doi:10.1177/1748895813483760.

Battle, F. (1999). *Measuring performance in the organized crime drug enforcement task force program*. Dissertation, University of Southern California.

Bayley, D. H. (1994). *Police for the future*. New York: Oxford University Press.

Beedle, S. (1984). *Citizen response to burglary information brochures: A follow-up study*. Portland: Public Affairs Unit, Crime Prevention Section, Portland Police Bureau.

Beetham, D. (1991). *The legitimation of power*. London: MacMillan.

Bennett, S., Denning, R., Mazerolle, L., & Stocks, B. (2009). *Procedural justice: A systematic literature search and technical report to the National Policing Improvement Agency*. Brisbane: Australian Research Council Centre of Excellence in Policing and Security.

Bennett, T. (1990). Getting back in touch. *Policing, 6*(3), 510–522.

Berringer, R. D. (2004). *The effect of formal leadership training on the leadership styles of police field trainers*. Prince Edward Island: University of Prince Edward Island.

Birzer, M. L. (1999). Police training in the 21st century. *FBI Law Enforcement Bulletin, 68*(7), 16–19.

Birzer, M. L. (2003). The theory of andragogy applied to police training. *Policing: An International Journal of Police Strategies & Management, 26*(1), 29–42. doi:10.1108/13639510310460288.

Bittner, E. (1974). Florence Nightingale in pursuit of Willie Sutton: A theory of the police. In H. Jacob (Ed.), *The potential for reform of criminal justice*. Thousand Oaks: Sage.

Blader, S. L., & Tyler, T. R. (2003). What constitutes fairness in work settings? A four-component model of procedural justice. *Human Resource Management Review, 13*(1), 107–126. doi:http://dx.doi.org/10.1016/S1053-4822(02)00101-8.

Bond, C. E. W., & Gow, D. J. (1997). Policing the beat: The experience in Toowoomba, Queensland. In R. Homel (Ed.), *Crime Prevention Studies Vol. 7. Policing for prevention: Reducing crime, public intoxication and injury* (Vol. 7, pp. 154–173). Monsey: Criminal Justice Press.

Bottoms, A., & Tankebe, J. (2012). Beyond procedural justice: A dialogic approach to legitimacy in criminal justice. *Journal of Criminal Law & Criminology, 102*(1), 120–170.

Bowling, B., Parmar, A., & Phillips, C. (2003). Policing ethnic minority communities. In T. Newburn (Ed.), *Handbook of policing* (pp. 528–555). Devon: Willan.

Bradford, B. (2012). Policing and social identity: Procedural justice, inclusion and cooperation between police and public. *Policing and Society,* 1–22. doi:10.1080/10439463.2012.724068.

Bradford, B., & Jackson, J. (2010). Different things to different people? The meaning and measurement of trust and confidence in policing across diverse social groups in London. *SSRN eLibrary*. doi:10.2139/ssrn.1628546.

L. Mazerolle et al., *Procedural Justice and Legitimacy in Policing*, SpringerBriefs in Criminology, DOI 10.1007/978-3-319-04543-6,

Bradford, B., Quinton, P., Myhill, A., & Porter, G. (2013). Why do 'the law' comply? Procedural justice, group identification and officer motivation in police organizations. *European Journal of Criminology*. doi:10.1177/1477370813491898.

Bradford, D., & Pynes, J. E. (1999). Police academy training: Why hasn't it kept up with practice? *Police Quarterly, 2*(3), 283–301. doi:10.1177/109861119900200302.

Braga, A. A. (2005). Hot spots policing and crime prevention: A systematic review of randomized controlled trials. *Journal of Experimental Criminology, 1*(3), 317–342.

Braga, A. A., & Weisburd, D. L. (2010). *Policing problem places: Crime hot spots and effective prevention* (Vol. Book, Whole). New York: Oxford University Press.

Braithwaite, J. (2002). *Restorative justice and responsive regulation*. Oxford: England Oxford University Press.

Braithwaite, J. (2010). *Anomie and violence: Non-truth and reconciliation in Indonesian peace-building*. Canberra: ANU E Press.

Brandl, S. G., Frank, J., Worden, R. E., & Bynum, T. S. (1994). Global and specific attitudes toward the police: Disentangling the relationship. *Justice Quarterly, 11*(1), 119–134. doi:10.1080/07418829400092161.

Brennan, M., & Brennan, R. (1994). *Cleartalk: Police responding to intellectual disability*. Wagga Wagga: Literacy Studies Network, School of Education, Charles Sturt University.

Brown, B., & Benedict, W. R. (2002). Perceptions of the police: Past findings, methodological issues, conceptual issues and policy implications. *Policing: An International Journal of Police Strategies & Management, 25*(3), 543–580.

Brownlee, I., & Walker, C. (1998). The urban crime fund and total geographic policing initiatives in West Yorkshire. *Policing and Society, 8*(2), 125–152.

Brunson, R. K., & Miller, J. (2006). Young black men and urban policing in the United States. *British Journal of Criminology, 46*, 613–640.

Buerger, M. E., Petrosino, A. J., & Petrosino, C. (1999). Extending the police role: Implications of police mediation as a problem-solving tool. *Police Quarterly, 2*(2), 125–149. doi:10.1177/109861119900200201.

Cherney, A., & Chui, W. (2009). Policing ethnically and culturally diverse communities. In A. Mulvane (Ed.), *Policing in context*. South Melbourne: Oxford University Press.

Cherney, A., & Head, B. (2011). Supporting the knowledge-to-action process: A systems-thinking approach. *Evidence & Policy, 7*(4), 471–488. doi:10.1332/174426411X603461.

Cherney, A., & Murphy, K. (2011). Understanding the contingency of procedural justice outcomes. *Policing, 5*(3), 228–235. doi:10.1093/police/par030.

Cherney, A., & Murphy, K. (2013). Policing terrorism with procedural justice: The role of police legitimacy and law legitimacy. *Australian & New Zealand Journal of Criminology*. doi:10.1177/0004865813485072.

Christakis, A., & Bausch, K. (2006). *How people harness their collective wisdom and power.* Charlotte: Information Age Publishing.

CiSocH (Civil Society Helpdesk) (2011, May 19). *Structured Dialogue Process: Part 1 & 2*. Paper presented at the Structured Dialogue for an Efficient Partnership in Development, Budapest, 19 May.

Cohen-Charash, Y., & Spector, P. E. (2001). The role of justice in organizations: A meta-analysis. *Organizational Behavior and Human Decision Processes, 86*(2), 278–321. doi:10.1006/obhd.2001.2958.

Coicaud, J. (2002). *Legitimacy and politics*. Cambridge: Cambridge University Press.

Colquitt, J. A. (2008). Two decades of organizational justice: Findings, controversies, and future directions. In J. Barling & C. L. Cooper (Eds.), *The Sage handbook of organizational behavior* (Vol. 1: Micro approaches, pp. 73–88). Newbury Park: Sage.

Colquitt, J. A., Conlon, D. E., Wesson, M. J., Porter, C. O. L. H., & Ng, K. Y. (2001). Justice at the millennium: A meta-analytic review of 25 years of organizational justice research. *Journal of Applied Psychology, 86*(3), 425–445. doi:10.1037/0021-9010.86.3.425.

Corcoran, J., & Allen, S. (2005). The effects of a police/victim assistance crisis team approach to domestic violence. *Journal of Family Violence, 20*(1), 39–45.

Cordner, G. W. (1998). Community policing: Elements and effect. In G. P. A. A. Piquero (Ed.), *Community policing: Contemporary readings* (pp. 45–62). Prospect Heights: Waveland Press.

Cosgrove, F., & Ramshaw, P. (2013). It is what you do as well as the way that you do it: The value and deployment of PCSOs in achieving public engagement. *Policing and Society,* 1–20. doi:10.1080/10439463.2013.802787.

Cropanzano, R., & Ambrose, M. L. (2001). Procedural and distributive justice are more similar than you think: A monistic perspective and a research agenda. In J. Greenberg & R. Cropanzano (Eds.), *Advances in organizational justice* (pp. 119-151). Stanford: Stanford University Press.

Dai, M. (2007). *Procedural justice during police-citizen encounters*. Doctoral dissertation, University of Cincinatti. Retrieved from ProQuest Dissertations & Theses (UMI Number: 3280116).

Dai, M., Frank, J., & Sun, I. (2011). Procedural justice during police-citizen encounters: The effects of process-based policing on citizen compliance and demeanor. *Journal of Criminal Justice, 39*(2), 159–168.

Davis, D. A., & Taylor-Vaisey, A. (1997). Translating guidelines into practice. A systematic review of theoretic concepts, practical experience and research evidence in the adoption of clinical practice guidelines. *CMAJ: Canadian Medical Association Journal* (*Journal de l'Association medicale canadienne*), *157*(4), 408–416.

Davis, R. C., & Lurigio, A. J. (1996). *Fighting back: Neighborhood antidrug strategies*. Thousand Oaks: Sage.

Davis, R. C., & Taylor, B. G. (1997). A proactive response to family violence: The results of a randomized experiment. *Criminology, 35*(2), 307–333.

Dickinson, A. (2010, April 21). Police ask drivers at RBTs whether they are being friendly enough. Bowen Hills: *The Courier Mail.*

Dixon, D. (1997). *Law in policing: legal regulation and police practices* (Vol. Book, Whole). Oxford: Clarendon Press.

Dogutas, C. (2007). *Reactive vs. proactive strategies: The effectivenss of school resource officers to prevent violence in schools*. Dissertation, Kent State University.

Dunworth, T., & Mills, G. (1999a). *National evaluation of weed and seed: Akron, Ohio research report*. Washington, DC: National Institute of Justice.

Dunworth, T., & Mills, G. (1999b). *National evaluation of weed and seed: Hartford, Connecticut research report*. Washington, DC: National Institute of Justice.

Dunworth, T., & Mills, G. (1999c). *National evaluation of weed and seed: Las Vegas, Nevada research report*. Washington, DC: National Institute of Justice.

Easton, D. (1958). The perception of authority and political change. In C. J. Friedruch (Ed.), *Authority*. Cambridge: Harvard University Press.

Elliott, I., Thomas, S. D. M., & Ogloff, J. R. P. (2011). Procedural justice in contacts with the police: the perspective of victims of crime. *Police Practice and Research,* 1–13. doi:10.1080/15614263.2011.607659.

European Commission. (2012). Structured dialogue for an efficient partnership in development. http://ec.europa.eu/europeaid/who/partners/civil-society/structured-dialogue_en.htm. Accessed 11 July 2013.

Flaspohler, P., Duffy, J., Wandersman, A., Stillman, L., & Maras, M. (2008). Unpacking prevention capacity: An intersection of research-to-practice models and community-centered models. *American Journal of Community Psychology, 41*(3–4), 182–196. doi:10.1007/s10464-008-9162-3.

Friday, P. C., Lord, V. B., Exum, M. L., & Hartman, J. L. (2006). Evaluating the impact of a specialized domestic violence police unit. In D. o. C. Justice. (Ed.). Charlotte: University of North Carolina.

Friedman, L. (1975). *The legal system: A social science perspective*. New York: Russell Sage.

Garland, D. (2001). *The culture of control: Crime and social order in contemporary society* (Vol. Book, Whole). Chicago: University of Chicago Press.

Gau, J. M., & Brunson, R. K. (2010). Procedural justice and order maintenance policing: A study of inner-city young men's perceptions of police legitimacy. *Justice Quarterly, 27*(2), 255–279.

Gerstein, R. (1970). The practice of fidelity to law. *Law and Society Review, 4,* 479–493.

Glover, E. (2007). Real principals listen. *Educational Leadership, 65,* 60–63.

Goldkamp, J. S., & Vilcica, E. R. (2008). Targeted enforcement and adverse system side effects: The generation of fugitives in Philadelphia. *Criminology, 46*(2), 371–409.

Goldsmith, A. (2005). Police reform and the problem of trust. *Theoretical Criminology, 9*(4), 443–470. doi:10.1177/1362480605057727.

Goldstein, H. (1990). *Problem-oriented policing.* New York: McGraw-Hill.

Goodman-Delahunty, J. (2010). Four ingredients: New recipes for procedural justice in Australian policing. *Policing, 4*(4), 403–410. doi:10.1093/police/paq041.

Graziano, L. M., Rosenbaum, D. P., & Schuck, A. M. (2013). Building group capacity for problem solving and police–community partnerships through survey feedback and training: A randomized control trial within Chicago's community policing program. *Journal of Experimental Criminology,* 1–25. doi:10.1007/s11292-012-9171-y.

Greene, J. R. (2000). Community policing in America: Changing the nature, structure, and function of the police. *Criminal Justice 2000: Policies, Processes, and Decisions of the Criminal Justice System, 3,* 299–370.

Greenhalgh, T., Robert, G., MacFarlane, F., Bate, P., & Kyriakidou, O. (2004). 'Diffusion of innovations in service organizations: Systematic review and recommendations'. *The Milbank Quarterly, 82*(2), 581–629.

Hanewicz, W. B., Fransway, L. M., & O'Neill, M. W. (1982). Improving the linkages between community mental health and the police. *Journal of Police Science and Administration, 10*(2), 218–223.

Hartstone, E. C., & Richetelli, D. M. (2003). *Final assessment of the strategic approaches to community safety initiative in New Haven.* Washington, DC: National Institute of Justice.

Hartstone, E. C., & Richetelli, D. M. (2005). Final assessment of the strategic approaches to community safety initiative in New Haven. In N. I. o. Justice (Ed.). Washington, DC: National Institute of Justice.

Harvey, J. (2005). Communities in conversation: Facilitating dialogue. CED Technique Paper.

Hawdon, J. E. (2008). Legitimacy, trust, social capital, and policing styles: A theoretical statement. *Police Quarterly, 11,* 182–201.

Henderson, C., Papagapiou, P., Gains, A., & Knox, J. (2004). *Driving crime down: Denying criminals the use of the road.* London: PA Consulting Group.

Hinds, L. (2009). Youth, police legitimacy and informal contact. *Journal of Police and Criminal Psychology, 24,* 10–21.

Hinds, L., & Murphy, T. (2007). Public satisfaction with police: Using procedural justice to improve police legitimacy. *Australian and New Zealand Journal of Criminology, 40*(1), 27–42.

Hogan, K., & Stubbs, R. (2003). *Can't get through: Eight barriers to communication.* Louisiana: Pelican Publishing Company, Inc.

Hohl, K., Bradford, B., & Stanko, E. A. (2010). Influencing trust and confidence in the London metropolitan police. *British Journal of Criminology, 50,* 491–513.

Holmberg, L. (2005). Policing and the feeling of safety: The rise (and fall?) of community policing in the Nordic countries. *Journal of Scandinavian Studies in Criminology and Crime Prevention, 5*(2), 205–219.

Homel, R. (1988). Deterernce-based policies in Britain, Canada and Australia. In M. D. Lawrence, J. R. Snortum & F. E. Zimring (Eds.), *The Social Control of Drinking and Driving* (pp. 64-78). Chicago: University of Chicago Press.

Hough, M. (2013). Procedural justice and professional policing in times of austerity. *Criminology and Criminal Justice, 13*(2), 181–197. doi:10.1177/1748895812466399.

Hovell, M. F., Seid, A. G., & Liles, S. (2006). Evaluation of a police and social services domestic violence program: Empirical evidence needed to inform public health policies. *Violence against women, 12*(2), 137–159.

Hoyle, C., Young, R., & Hill, R. (2002). *Proceed with caution: An evaluation of the Thames Valley Police initiative in restorative cautioning.* York: Joseph Rowntree Foundation.

Huo, Y. J. (2003). Procedural justice and social regulation across group boundaries: Does subgroup identity undermine relationship-based governance? *Personality and Social Psychology Bulletin, 29,* 336–348.

Isaacs, W. N. (1999). Dialogic leadership. *The Systems Thinker, 10*(1), 1–5.

Jackson, J., & Bradford, B. (2009). Crime, policing and social order: On the expressive nature of public confidence in policing. *The British Journal of Sociology, 60*(3), 493–521. doi:10.1111/j.1468-4446.2009.01253.x.

Jackson, J., Bradford, B., Hough, M., Myhill, A., Quinton, P., & Tyler, T. R. (2012). Why do people comply with the law? Legitimacy and the influence of legal institutions. *British Journal of Criminology, 52,* 1051–1071. doi:10.1093/bjc/azs032.

Jackson, J., Bradford, B., Stanko, B., & Hohl, K. (2013). *Just authority? Trust in the police in England and Wales* (Vol. Book, Whole). Milton Park: Routledge.

Kane, R. J. (2005). Compromised police legitimacy as a predictor of violent crime in structurally disadvantaged communities. *Criminology, 43*(2), 469–498.

Katz, C. M. (1997). *Police and gangs: A study of a police gang unit.* Dissertation.

Kelling, G. L., & Moore, M. H. (1988). The evolving strategy of police *Perspectives on Policing, 4,* 1–16.

Kerley, K. R., & Benson, M. L. (2000). Does community-oriented policing help build stronger communities? *Police Quarterly, 3*(1), 46–69.

Kochel, T. R. (2011). Constructing hot spots policing: Unexamined consequences for disadvantaged populations and for police legitimacy. *Criminal Justice Policy Review, 22*(3), 350–374.

Kubrin, C. E., & Weitzer, R. (2003). New directions in social disorganization theory. *Journal of Research in Crime and Delinquency, 40*(4), 374–402.

Lambert, R. (2011). *Countering Al-Qaeda in London: Police and Muslims in partnership* (Vol. Book, Whole). London: Hurst & Company.

Lardner, R. (1992, July). Factors affecting police/social work inter-agency co-operation in a child protection unit. *The Police Journal,* 213–228.

Lipsey, M. W., & Wilson, D. B. (2001). *Practical meta-analysis* (Applied social research methods series; Vol. 49). Thousand Oaks: Sage.

MacCoun, R. J. (2005). Voice, control, and belonging: The double-edged sword of procedural fairness. In *Annual Review of Law and Social Science* (Vol. 1, pp. 171–201, Annual Review of Law and Social Science).

Manning, P. K. (1977). *Police work: The social organization of policing* (Vol. Book, Whole). Cambridge: MIT Press.

Marshall, T. F. (1999). Restorative justice: An overview. In H. Office (Ed.). United Kingdom: HM Government.

Martin, P. (2012a). Interview conducted by Adrian Cherney. Transcription. Brisbane.

Martin, P. (2012b). Zooming in on PJ Dialogue. Personal account of the dialogue development of QCET. Brisbane.

Mastrofski, S. D. (Ed.). (2006). *Community policing: A skeptical view (Police Innovation: Contrasting Perspectives).* Cambridge: Cambridge University Press.

Mastrofski, S. D., Snipes, J. B., & Supina, A. E. (1996). Compliance on demand: The public's response to specific police requests. *Journal of Research in Crime and Delinquency, 33*(3), 269–305. doi:10.1177/0022427896033003001.

Matthews, R. (1993). Kerb-crawling, prostitution and multi-agency policing. *Crime Prevention Unit Series Paper No. 43.* London: Home Office Police Department, Police Research Group.

Mazerolle, L., Antrobus, E., Bennett, S., & Tyler, T. R. (2013a). Shaping citizen perceptions of police legitimacy: A randomized field trial of procedural justice. *Criminology, 51*(1), 33–63. doi:10.1111/j.1745-9125.2012.00289.x.

Mazerolle, L., Bates, L., Bennett, S., White, G., Ferris, J., & Antrobus, E. (in preparation). Optimising the length of Random Breath Tests: Results from the Queensland Community Engagement Trial.

Mazerolle, L., Bennett, S., Antrobus, E., & Eggins, L. (2011a). *Key findings of the Queensland Community Engagement Trial* (Briefing Paper). Brisbane: ARC Centre of Excellence in Policing and Security.

Mazerolle, L., Bennett, S., Antrobus, E., & Eggins, L. (2012). Procedural justice, routine encounters and citizen perceptions of police: Main findings from the Queensland Community Engagement Trial (QCET). *Journal of Experimental Criminology, 8*(4), 343–367. doi:10.1007/s11292-012-9160-1.

Mazerolle, L., Bennett, S., Davis, J., Sargeant, E., & Manning, M. (2013b). Legitimacy in policing: A systematic review. *Campbell Systematic Reviews, 1*. doi:10.4073/csr.2013.1.

Mazerolle, L., Bennett, S., Eggins, L., Antrobus, E., White, G., & Davis, J. (2011b). *Testing police legitimacy...one breath at a time: The Queensland Community Engagement Trial (QCET) (Technical Report).* Brisbane: ARC Centre of Excellence in Policing and Security.

Mazerolle, L., & Ransley, J. (2005). *Third party policing*. Cambridge: Cambridge University Press.

McCluskey, J. D. (2003). *Police requests for compliance: Coercive and procedurally just tactics*. New York: LFB Scholarly Publishing.

Mccluskey, J. D., Mastrofski, S. D., & Parks, R. B. (1999). To Acquiesce or rebel: Predicting citizen compliance with police requests. *Police Quarterly, 2*(4), 389–416. doi:10.1177/109861119900200401.

McCold, P. (2003). An experiment in police-based restorative justice: The Bethlehem (Pennsylvania) Project. *Police Practice & Research, 4*(4), 379–390.

McCold, P., & Wachtel, B. (1998). The Bethlehem Pennsylvania Police Family Group Conferencing Project. Pipersville, PA: Community Service Foundation.

McDevitt, J., Farrell, A., & Wolff, R. (2008). *COPS Evaluation Brief No. 3: Creating a culture of integrity*. Washington, DC: Office of Community Oriented Policing Services, US Department of Justice.

McGarrell, E. F., & Chermak, S. (2004a). Strategic approaches to reducing firearms violence: Final report on the Indianapolis violence reduction partnership. Washington, DC: United States Department of Justice, National Institute of Justice.

McGarrell, E. F., & Chermak, S. (2004b). Strategic approaches to reducing firearms violence: Final report on the Indianapolis violence reduction partnership. In N. I. o. Justice. (Ed.). Washington, DC: National Institute of Justice.

Meredyth, D., McKernan, H., & Evans, R. (2010). Police and Vietnamese-Australian communities in multi-ethnic Melbourne. *Policing, 4*(3), 233–240. doi:10.1093/police/paq021.

Michael, D. R., Justice, T., & Gorazd, M. (2012). Procedural justice, police legitimacy, and public cooperation with the police among young Slovene adults. *Varstvoslovje, 14*(2), 147.

Moon, B., McCluskey, J., & Lee, S. (2005). Korean police officers' attitudes toward the efficacy of mini-police stations. *Journal of Criminal Justice, 33*(5), 441–449.

Moore, D. B., & O'Connell, T. (1994). Family Conferencing in Wagga Wagga: A Communitarian Model of Justice. In C. Alder, & J. Wundersitz (Eds.), *Family conferencing and juvenile justice: The way forward or misplaced optimism?* (pp. 15–44). Canberra: Australian Institute of Criminology.

Morrell, G., Scott, S., McNeish, D., & Webster, S. (2011). The august riots in England: Understanding the involvement of young people. In t. C. Office (Ed.). London: NatCen.

Murphy, K. (2009). Public satisfaction with police: The importance of procedural justice and police performance in police-citizen encounters. *Australian & New Zealand Journal of Criminology, 42*(2), 159–178. doi:10.1375/acri.42.2.159.

Murphy, K. (2013). Policing at the margins: Fostering trust and cooperation among ethnic minority groups. *Journal for Policing, Intelligence and Counter Terrorism, 8*(2), 184–199.

Murphy, K., & Cherney, A. (2011). Fostering cooperation with the police: How do ethnic minorities in Australia respond to procedural justice-based policing? *Australian & New Zealand Journal of Criminology, 44*(2), 235–257. doi:10.1177/0004865811405260.

Murphy, K., & Cherney, A. (2012). Understanding cooperation with police in a diverse society. *British Journal of Criminology, 52*(1), 181–201. doi:10.1093/bjc/azr065.

Murphy, K., Hinds, L., & Fleming, J. (2008). Encouraging public cooperation and support for police. *Policing and Society, 18*(2), 136–155.
Murphy, K., Mazerolle, L., & Bennett, S. (in press). Promoting trust in police: Findings from a randomized experimental field trial of procedural justice policing. *Policing and Society.*
Murphy, K., & Mearns, M. (2008). *The public safety and security in Australia survey: Survey methodology and preliminary findings*. ARC Centre for Excellence in Policing and Security Working Paper: The Australian National University.
Murphy, K., & Tyler, T. R. (2008). Procedural justice and compliance behaviour: The mediating role of emotions. *European Journal of Social Psychology, 38*(4), 652–668.
Murphy, K., Tyler, T. R., & Curtis, A. (2009). Nurturing regulatory compliance: Is procedural justice effective when people question the legitimacy of the law? *Regulation & Governance, 3,* 1–26.
Murray, B. J. (2003). *Perceptions of principals, school resource officers, and school resource officer supervisors of the School Resource Officer Program in comprehensive high schools in Riverside County, California*. Dissertation, University of La Verne,
Murray, T. (2007). Police-building in Afghanistan: A case study of civil security reform'. *International Peacekeeping, 17,* 108–126.
Myhill, A. (2006). *Community engagement in policing: Lessons from the literature*. London: Home Office.
Myhill, A., & Bradford, B. (2013). Overcoming cop culture? Organizational justice and police officers' attitudes toward the public. *Policing: An International Journal of Police Strategies & Management, 36*(2), 338–356. doi:10.1108/13639511311329732.
Noblet, A. J., & Rodwell, J. J. (2008). Integrating job stress and social exchange theories to predict employee strain in reformed public sector contexts. *Journal of Public Administration Research and Theory, 19,* 555–575.
Noblet, A. J., Rodwell, J. J., & Allisey, A. F. (2009). Police stress: The role of the psychological contract and perceptions of fairness. *Policing: An International Journal of Police Strategies & Management, 32*(4), 613–630.
Novak, K. J., Hartman, J. L., Holsinger, A. M., & Turner, M. G. (1999). The effects of aggressive policing of disorder on serious crime. *Policing: An International Journal of Police Strategies & Management, 22*(2), 171–190. doi:10.1108/13639519910271229.
Paoline, E. A. (2004). Shedding light on police culture: An examination of officers' occupational attitudes. *Police Quarterly, 7*(2), 205–236. doi:10.1177/1098611103257074.
Pate, A. M., & Annan, S. O. (1989). *The Baltimore community policing experiment: Summary report*. Washington, DC: Police Foundation.
Paternoster, R., Brame, R., Bachman, R., & Sherman, L. W. (1997). Do fair procedures matter? The effect of procedural justice on spouse assault. *Law & Society Review, 31*(1), 163–204. doi:10.2307/3054098.
Pease, A., & Pease, B. (1994). *The definitive book of body language*. United Kingdom: Orion Books.
Penfold, C., Hunter, G., Campbell, R., & Barham, L. (2004). Tackling client violence in female street prostitution: Inter-agency working between outreach agencies and the police. *Policing and Society, 14*(4), 365–379.
Pickering, S. J., McCulloch, J., & Wright-Neville, D. P. (2008). *Counter-terrorism policing: Community, cohesion and security*. USA: Springer.
Police Executive Research Forum (2013). *Policing and the Economic Downturn: Striving for Efficiency In the New Normal*. Paper presented at the Critical Issues in Policing Series, Washington, DC.
Queensland Police Service. (2012). *Annual Report: Queensland police service*. Brisbane: State of Queensland—Queensland Police Service.
Quinton, P., Mills, A., & Wheller, L. (2012, July 9–11). *The Greater Manchester Police Procedural Justice Training Experiment*. Paper presented at the 5th International Conference on Evidence-Based Policing, University of Cambridge.
Reisig, M. D. (2010). Community and problem-oriented policing. *Crime and Justice, 39*(1), 1–53.

Reisig, M. D., Bratton, J., & Gertz, M. G. (2007). The construct validity and refinement of process-based policing measures. *Criminal Justice and Behavior, 34*(8), 1005–1028.

Ren, L., Cao, L., Lovrich, N., & Gaffney, M. (2005). Linking confidence in police with the performance of the police: Community policing can make a difference. *Journal of Criminal Justice, 33,* 55–66.

Reuss-Ianni, E. (1993). *Two cultures of policing: Street cops and management cops*. New Brunswick: Transaction Publishers.

Röder, A., & Mühlau, P. (2012). What determines the trust of immigrants in criminal justice institutions in Europe? *European Journal of Criminology, 9*(4), 370–387. doi:10.1177/1477370812447265.

Rogers, E. M. (1995). *Diffusion of innovations* (4th ed.). New York: The Free Press.

Rosenbaum, D. P. (2006). *The limits of hot spots policing (Police innovation: Contrasting perspectives)*. Cambridge: Cambridge University Press.

Rosenbaum, D. P., & Lawrence, D. S. (2013). Teaching respectful police-citizen encounters and good decision making: Results of a randomized control trial with police recruits. Report for the National Police Research Platform. http://www.nationalpoliceresearch.org/the-chicago-quality-interactio/.

Roth, J. A., Ryan, J. F., Gaffigan, S. J., Koper, C. S., Moore, M. H., Roehl, J. A., et al (2000). *National evaluation of the COPS Program—Title I of the 1994 Crime Act*. Washington, DC: National Institute of Justice, Office of Justice Programs, US Department of Justice.

Rubenser, L. L. (2000). *Special units in policing: A case study of a nuisance task force*. Dissertation, University of Nebraska, University of Nebraska.

Sadd, S., & Grinc, R. (1994). Innovative neighborhood-oriented policing: An evaluation of community policing programs in eight cities. In D. P. Rosenbaum (Ed.), *The challenge of community policing: Testing the promises* (pp. 27-52). London: Sage.

Sargeant, E., Murphy, K., & Cherney, A. (in press). Ethnicity, trust and cooperation with police: Testing the dominance of the process-based model. *European Journal of Criminology*.

Saunders, M. N. K., & Thornhill, A. (2003). Organisational justice, trust and the management of change – An exploration. *Personnel Review, 32*(3), 360–375. doi:10.1108/00483480310467660.

Scheingold, S. A. (1984). *The politics of law and order: street crime and public policy* (Vol. Book, Whole). Quid Pro, LLC.

Schmitz, R., Wassenberg, P. S., Gransky, L., Hagner, P. G., & Sims, P. L. (1998). *An evaluation of the homicide and violent crime strike force program in Madison and St. Clair counties*. Springfield: Center for Legal Studies, Institute for Public Affairs, University of Illinois.

Schuck, A. M., & Rosenbaum, D. P. (2011). *The Chicago quality interaction training program: A randomized control trial of police innovation* (Vol. 28). Washington, DC: National Police Research Platform, National Institute of Justice.

Schulhofer, S. J., Tyler, T. R., & Huq, A. Z. (2011). American policing at a crossroads: Unsustainable policies and the procedural justice alternative. *Journal of Criminal Law & Criminal Justice, 2,* 335–374.

Scott, J. (1998). 'Performance culture': The return of reactive policing. *Policing and Society, 8*(3), 269–288. doi:10.1080/10439463.1998.9964792.

Scott, M. S. (2000). *Problem-oriented policing: Reflections on the first 20 years (Office of Community Oriented Policing Services, Trans.)*. Washington, DC: U.S. Department of Justice.

Scott, M. S. (2004). *The benefits and consequences of police crackdowns (Problem-Oriented Guides for Police Response Guides Series Guide No. 1)*. Washington, DC: Community Oriented Policing Services.

Scott, M. S., & Kirby, S. (2012). *Implementing POP: Leading, structuring, and managing a problem-oriented police agency*. Washington, DC: Office of Community Oriented Policing Services.

Sellers, C. S., Taylor, T. J., & Esbensen, F.-A. (1998). Reality check: Evaluating a school-based gang prevention model. *Evaluation Review, 22*(5), 590–608.

Shapland, J., Atkinson, A., Atkinson, H., Colledge, E., Dignan, J., Howes, M., et al (2006). Situating restorative justice within criminal justice. *Theoretical Criminology, 10*(4), 505–532. doi:10.1177/1362480606068876.

Shapland, J., Atkinson, A., Atkinson, H., Dignan, J., Edwards, L., Hibbert, J., et al. (2008). *Does restorative justice affect reconviction? The fourth report from the evaluation of three schemes. Ministry of Justice Research Series* (Vol. 10). London: Ministry of Justice.

Sherman, L. W. (Ed.). (1990). *Police Crackdowns: Initital and residual deterrence (Vol. 12, Crime and Justice: An Annual Review of Research)*. Chicago: University of Chicago Press.

Sherman, L. W. (1993). Defiance, deterrence, and irrelevance: A theory of the criminal sanction. *Journal of Research in Crime and Delinquency, 30*(4), 445–473. doi:10.1177/0022427893030004006.

Sherman, L. W. (1998). *Evidence-based policing*. Washington, DC: Police Foundation.

Sherman, L. W., Gartin, P. R., & Buerger, M. E. (1989). Hot spots of predatory crime: Routine activities and the criminology of place. *Criminology, 27*(1), 27–56.

Sherman, L. W., & Strang, H. (2007). *Restorative justice: The evidence. Report to the Smith Institute*. London: The Smith Institute.

Sherman, L. W., Strang, H., Barnes, G. C., Braithwaite, J., Inkpen, N., & Teh, M.-M. (1998). *Experiments in restorative policing: A progress report on the Canberra Reintegrative Shaming Experiments (RISE)*. Canberra: Australian Federal Police and Australian National University.

Sherman, L. W., & Weisburd, D. (1995). General deterrent effects of police patrol in crime "hot spots": A randomized, controlled trial. *Justice Quarterly, 12*(4), 625–648.

Silk, P. D., Spalek, B., & O'Rawe, M. (2013). *Preventing ideological violence: Communities, police and case studies of "Success"*. Palgrave Macmillan.

Singer, L. (2004). Reassurance policing: An evaluation of the local management of community safety. In H. O. R. Studies (Ed.), (Vol. 228). London: Home Office.

Skogan, W. G. (2006). Asymmetry in the impact of encounters with police. *Policing and Society, 16*(2), 99–126.

Skogan, W. G. (2008). Why reforms fail. *Policing and Society, 18*(1), 23–34.

Skogan, W. G., & Hartnett, S. M. (1997). *Community policing, Chicago Style*. New York: Oxford University Press.

Spalek, B. (2012). *Counter-terrorism: Community-based approaches to preventing terror crime* (Vol. Book, Whole). New York: Palgrave Macmillan.

Sun, I. Y., Wu, Y., & Poteyeva, M. (2011). Arab Americans' opinion on counterterrorism measures: The impact of race, ethnicity, and religion. *Studies in Conflict & Terrorism, 34*(7), 540–555. doi:10.1080/1057610X.2011.578550.

Sunshine, J., & Tyler, T. R. (2003). The role of procedural justice and legitimacy in shaping public support for policing. *Law & Society Review, 37*(3), 513–548.

Sykes, R. E., & Clark, J. P. (1975). A theory of deference Exchange in police-civilian encounters. *American Journal of Sociology, 81*(3), 584–600. doi:10.2307/2777645.

Tankebe, J. (2008). Colonialism, legitimation, and policing in Ghana. *International Journal of Law, Crime and Justice, 36*(1), 67–84. doi:http://dx.doi.org/10.1016/j.ijlcj.2007.12.003.

Tankebe, J. (2009a). Policing, procedural fairness and public behaviour: A review and ctitique. *International Journal of Police Science & Management, 11*(1), 8–19.

Tankebe, J. (2009b). Public cooperation with the police in Ghana: Does procedural fairness matter? *Criminology, 47*(4), 1265–1293. doi:10.1111/j.1745-9125.2009.00175.x.

Tankebe, J. (2013). In search of moral recognition? Policing and eudaemonic legitimacy in Ghana. *Law & Social Inquiry, 38*(3), 576–597. doi:10.1111/lsi.12025.

Taylor, N., & Charlton, K. (2005). *Police shopfronts and reporting to police by retailers. Trends and Issues in crime and criminal justice No. 295. Canberra*. Australia: Australian Institute of Criminology.

Tennant, W. A. (1986). *Police management of dangerous mentally disturbed individuals through proactive intervention*. Dissertation, Wright Institute.

Tilley, N., & Pawson, R. (1997). *Realistic evaluation* (Vol. Book, Whole). Thousand Oaks: Sage.

Toch, H. (2008). Police officers as change agents in police reform. *Policing and Society, 18*(1), 60–71. doi:10.1080/10439460701718575.

Tuffin, R., Morris, J., & Poole, A. (2006). *An evaluation of the impact of the National Reassurance Policing programme. Home Office Research Study 296*. London: Development and Statistics Directorate, Home Office Research.

Turnbull, P. J., Webster, R., & Stiliwell, G. (1996). Get it while you can: An evaluation of an early intervention project for arrestees with alcohol and drug problems. In H. O. D. P. Initiative (Ed.). London: Home Office Drugs Prevention Initiative.

Tyler, T. R. (1990). *Why people obey the law*. New Haven: Yale University Press.

Tyler, T. R. (1997). *Social justice in a diverse society*. Boulder: Westview.

Tyler, T. R. (2000). Multiculturalism and the willingness of citizens to defer to law and to legal authorities. *Law & Social Inquiry, 25*(4), 983–1019.

Tyler, T. R. (2001a). A psychological perspective on the legitimacy of institutions and authorities. In J. Jost & B. Major (Eds.), *The psychology of legitimacy*. Cambridge: Cambridge University Press.

Tyler, T. R. (2001b). Public trust and confidence in legal authorities: What do majority and minority group members want from the law and legal institutions? *Behavioral Sciences and the Law, 19,* 215–235.

Tyler, T. R. (2003). Procedural justice, legitimacy, and the effective rule of law. In M. H. Tonry (Ed.), *Crime and Justice: A Review of Research,* Chicago: University of Chicago Press.

Tyler, T. R. (2004). Enhancing Police Legitimacy. *Annals of the American Academy of Political and Social Science, 593,* 84–99.

Tyler, T. R. (2006a). Restorative Justice and Procedural Justice: Dealing with rule breaking. *Journal of Social Issues, 62*(2), 307–326.

Tyler, T. R. (2006b). *Why people obey the law*. New Haven: Princeton University Press.

Tyler, T. R. (2008). Procedural justice and the courts. *Court Review, 44,* 25–31.

Tyler, T. R., & Fagan, J. (2008). Legitimacy and cooperation: Why do people help the police fight crime in their communities? *Ohio State Journal of Criminal Law, 6,* 231–276.

Tyler, T. R., & Huo, Y. J. (2002). *Trust in the law*. New York: Russell Sage.

Tyler, T. R., & Lind, E. A. (1992). A relational model of authority in groups. *Advances in Eexperimental Social Psychology, 25,* 115–191.

Tyler, T. R., Lind, E. A., & Huo, Y. J. (2000). Cultural values and authority relations: The psychology of conflict resolution across cultures. *Psychology, Public Policy, and Law, 6*(4), 1138–1163. doi:10.1037/1076-8971.6.4.1138.

Tyler, T. R., Schulhofer, S., & Huq, A. Z. (2010). Legitimacy and deterrence effects in counterterrorism policing: A study of Muslim Americans. *Law & Society Review, 44*(2), 365–402.

Tyler, T. R., & Wakslak, C. (2004). Profiling and the legitimacy of the police: Procedural justice, attributions of motive, and the acceptance of social authority. *Criminology, 42,* 13–42.

Volpe, M. R., & Phillips, N. (2003). Police use of mediation. *Conflict Resolution Quarterly, 21*(2), 263–267.

Van Craen, M. (2012a). Determinants of ethnic minority confidence in the police. *Journal of Ethnic and Migration Studies, 38*(7), 1029–1047. doi: 10.1080/1369183X.2012.681447.

Van Craen, M. (2012b). Explaining majority and minority trust in the police. *Justice Quarterly,* 1–26. doi: 10.1080/07418825.2011.649295

Walker, S. (1992). *The police in America* (2nd ed.). New York: McGraw-Hill.

Walzer, M. (1994). *Thick and thin: Moral arguments at home and abroad.* Notre Dame: University of Notre Dame Press.

Warren, P. Y. (2010). The continuing significance of race: An analysis across two levels of policing. *Social Science Quarterly, 91*(4), 1025–1042. doi:10.1111/j.1540-6237.2010.00747.x.

Watson, A. C., Angell, B., Vidalon, T., & Davis, K. (2010). Measuring perceived procedural justice and coercion among persons with mental illness in police encounters: The police contact experience scale. *Journal of Community Psychology, 38*(2), 206–226. doi:10.1002/jcop.20360.

Weber, M. (1978). *Economy and society* (Vol. 1). Los Angeles: University of California Press.

Weisburd, D., & Eck, J. E. (2004). What can police do to reduce crime, disorder, and fear? *The Annals of the American Academy of Political and Social Science, 593,* 42–65.

Weisburd, D., Hinkle, J., Famega, C., & Ready, J. (2011). The possible "backfire" effects of hot spots policing: An experimental assessment of impacts on legitimacy, fear and collective efficacy. *Journal of Experimental Criminology, 7*(4), 297–320.

Weisburd, D., Maher, L., & Sherman, L. W. (Eds.). (1992). *Contrasting crime general and crime specific theory: The case of hot spots of crime (Advances in Criminological Theory)*. New Brunswick: Transaction.

Weisburd, D., Morris, N. A., & Ready, J. (2008). Risk-focused policing at places: An experimental evaluation. *Justice Quarterly, 25*(1), 163–200.

Weitzer, R., & Tuch, S. A. (2006). *Race and policing in America: Conflict and reform*. New York: Cambridge University Press.

Welsh, B., Sullivan, C., & Olds, D. (2010). When early crime prevention goes to scale: A new look at the evidence. *Prevention Science, 11*(2), 115–125. doi:10.1007/s11121-009-0159-4.

Wenzel, M., Okimoto, T. G., Feather, N. T., & Platow, M. J. (2008). Retributive and restorative justice. *Law and Human Behaviour, 32*(5), 375–389. doi:http://dx.doi.org/10.1007/s10979-007-9116-6.

Wheller, L., Quinton, P., Fildes, A., & Mills, A. (2013). The Greater Manchester Police procedural justice training experiment: The impact of commuication skills training on officers and victims of crime. London: College of Policing. http://www.college.police.uk/en/docs/Practitioner_Paper_Final.pdf.

White, M. D., Fyfe, J. J., Campbell, S. P., & Goldkamp, J. S. (2001). The school-police partnership: Identifying at-risk youth through a Truant Recovery Program. *Evaluation Review, 25*(5), 507–532.

Winfree, L. T. J., Lynskey, D. P., & Maupin, J. R. (1999). Developing local police and federal law enforcement partnerships: G.R.E.A.T. as a case study of policy implementation. *Criminal Justice Review, 24*(2), 145–168.

Wolfe, S. E., & Piquero, A. R. (2011). Organizational justice and police misconduct. *Criminal Justice and Behavior, 38*(4), 332–353. doi:10.1177/0093854810397739.

MIX
Papier aus verantwortungsvollen Quellen
Paper from responsible sources
FSC® C105338

If you have any concerns about our products,
you can contact us on
ProductSafety@springernature.com

In case Publisher is established outside the EU,
the EU authorized representative is:
Springer Nature Customer Service Center GmbH
Europaplatz 3, 69115 Heidelberg, Germany

Printed by Libri Plureos GmbH
in Hamburg, Germany